LACROSSE
THE GLOBE

LACROSSE THE GLOBE

NICHOLAS MARROCCO

NEW DEGREE PRESS

LACROSSE THE GLOBE

ISBN-13 978-1978455955

CONTENTS

———

INTRODUCTION: WORLD LACROSSE CHAMPIONSHIP:
JAPAN VS. KENYA SCORE AND FINAL RECAP 1

1. FINLAND 19 COLOMBIA 0 17

2. MY JOURNEY TO LACROSSE 38

3. FACILITATING YOUTH LEAGUES 56

4. LIVING LIFE AS A LACROSSE PLAYER 79

5. THE IMG EXPERIENCE 95

6. REALITY CHECK 112

7. THE COLLEGE DREAM 125

8. HOW RUSSIA CREATED A DOMINATING SPORTS
   PROGRAM—THAT ANOTHER COUNTRY COULD
   MODEL THEIR PROGRAMS ON 139

9. THE NEW VISION.. 152

ACKNOWLEDGEMENTS.. 170

SOURCES USED... 172

WORLD LACROSSE CHAMPIONSHIP: JAPAN VS. KENYA SCORE AND FINAL RECAP

———

Marian Lopacek JULY 19th

"We knew this was our chance to shock the world and win our first World Cup," said coach Yoshihiro Okubo. "And boy did we."

There are few things across the sports landscape that get players and fans more fired up than a showdown with a bitter rival. Those feelings become even more intensified when those rivals meet up with everything on the line.

That is exactly what happened at the World Lacrosse Championship game Saturday near Warsaw, Poland. Japan knocked off its archrival, Kenya, in a game that wasn't as close as the final score indicated, 8-5.

Tsugu Watura and Shinya Maruyama led the way for the Japanese, totaling five goals, but Hattori Shunsuke's effort in goal against the powerful Kenyan offense should not go overlooked. From the opening minutes, Japan controlled possession and was more than happy to bleed the clock with stall tactics on offense. The strategy worked to perfection, and Nozomi and the offense capitalized on opportunities when they presented themselves.

The Japanese team was led by young players but showed all the confidence in the world, making skilled plays left and right and proving they were meant to be there that championship day.

Playing on more athleticism than the skilled tactic of the Japanese, the Kenyan team was led by a very shifty and fast offense who moved the ball with great speed.

Despite this fast ball movement and terrific agility running upfield, the Japanese stick skills showed too strong to be beaten. What we have been told is that the Japanese have been crafting their indoor lacrosse game, which is the main reason for the Japanese National team's tremendous skills all over the field.

Just one game ago, Japan came up against the United States, a team who has dominated the World Games for decades now. Despite the United States having both skill and physique, the Japanese did not seem scared. Defender Yoshida Isao Takeshi showed no signs of weakness as he took on the very powerful Rob Pannell, a player known to put the ball in the back of the net nearly every time it touched his stick.

Jesse Schwartzman had a tremendous first half in the cage for the Americans, allowing 5 goals but totaling 9 saves. The Japanese changed their game plan in the second half, led by attacker Wataru Tsugu who sat behind the net patiently and found several of his teammates wide open on the crease. Quick ball movement and smart play from the Japanese attack unit put 8 goals in the back of the net in the second half of this game to secure a 12-7 win.

The Kenyan athleticism was something the Japanese were just not used to seeing, creating much frustration for the Japanese midfielders as they were pressured all over the field. Coach Okubo called a timeout early into the second quarter to slow down the pace of the game and reassure his team of how they made it this far: their skills. This proved to be a smart move, as the Japanese controlled the ball for a majority of the rest of the game and secured their first World Games Championship!

———

The excitement of this World Championship Lacrosse match is real.

The teams?

Fiction.

Wait, why is this fiction?

In the past 50 years of the World Championships for lacrosse, only two teams have ever won:

The United States and Canada.

Just two. Japan, Kenya, Russia, China, France, England, and over forty other participating nations have never even come close.

But what if I told you that at some point in the future, it's entirely possible that we'll see a championship featuring two teams that will shock you? Yes, perhaps a Kenya-Japan final isn't impossible.

This is the story of how to create a Cinderella scenario. In numerous sports played around the globe, there have been Cinderella stories—stories of teams from nations without a long, respected history in a sport becoming a shocking participant and eventually a champion.

You may or may not have heard the stories of the Jamaican Bobsled team, a group who came from no money and ended up changing the way the sport was perceived.

The story begins with George Fitch, the man who co-founded the team. He was formerly the Commercial Attache for the American embassy in Kingston from 1985-86, before he was transferred to Paris. It was there that he developed a strong friendship with Ken Barnes, the father of former Liverpool star John Barnes. In June of 1987, at a friend's wedding, Barnes began bragging about how well Jamaica was going to do at the next summer's Olympics in Seoul. "But what about the winter Olympics?" Fitch responded. "You got great athletes and a great athlete should be able to do any sport". This got Fitch thinking about the possibilities, one of which would later be monumental for the winter Olympics and Jamaica. (Nick Atkin, ESPN)

Fitch began to think of what sport he could experiment with as the new winter sport for the Jamaicans. Bobsledding! The perfect sport that would play to Jamaica's sprinting strengths. Fitch explained his logic, stating that "Half the race is how quickly you can push a 600-pound object before you jump, and then the driver just lets the sled steer itself". How hard could it be?

Fitch began approaching some of the top Jamaican athletes who were training for Seoul but had been dismissed. But these athletes knew bobsledding was dangerous and chose not to take the risk. Next, he decided to try reaching out to the sports clubs in Kingston but again, nobody wanted to take part. Next up: open tryouts.

This tactic showed a lot of good and a lot of bad. The contenders varied from street vendors to fisherman to athletes. Luckily, Ken Barnes stepped up and played a huge role in recruiting talented members. Ken had Major George Henry from the Jamaica Defense Force there and when Fitch told Ken he needed speed to push the sleds, Ken looked over to George and said "Hey George, who's our current sprint champion?" The duo was Mike White and Devon Harris, Mike being the sprint champion and Devon being the 800 meters champion. When Fitch said he needed good hand-eye coordination to drive the sled, Ken responded, "Like a helicopter pilot?" Again, Ken turned to George and asked who their helicopter pilot was. So, Dudley Stokes, the helicopter pilot, and the two runners, Mike White and Devon Harris, formed the first three members of the Jamaica bobsled team.

For the three new members, this was an unusual and unexpected task to take on. Harris had a dream of going to the Seoul in '88, "But certainly not the Winter Olympics. To be honest when this came up I was thinking that this is ridiculous. But there I am."

Fitch used $92,000 of his own money to train, and sent the team to Austria to take part in a World Cup race to meet the international Bobsleigh and Skeleton Federation's (FIBT) requirements. Soon after qualifying, team members Dudley Stokes, Devon Harris and Michael White, alternates Freddie 'Reggae' Powell and Caswell Allen, coach Howard Sailer and George Fitch arrived in Calgary.

The plan was for the team to only take part in the two-man sled races, but after they beat 10 teams and had eight days remaining, they decided to give the four-man sled a try. But they had some immediate issues. Despite being happy with the results of the two-man sled races, Fitch saw big issues with the four-man attempt. "I told the guys, 'Let me just point out three problems, immediately'," says Fitch. "One, we've never really been in a four. Two, I'm totally out of money and nobody's going to loan us a sled. A sled's gonna cost about

$25,000 (£15,000). And three, I only count three guys sitting around in this room here." Freddie had gone "walkabout" as Fitch explained it, and Caswell fell on the track and got injured. In reality, his ego was hurt more than his body. So, Fitch made new plans. (ESPN)

Fitch made a deal in a Calgary bar to sell Jamaica bobsled t-shirts that his wife had made. They were a huge hit! Fitch made $24,000 on the t-shirts, enough to buy a four-man sled from the Canadian team. Next, they had to find a fourth member. Dudley told Fitch that his brother, Chris Stokes, was training on a track scholarship at the University of Idaho. Surprisingly, Fitch was able to convince an Olympic official to give Chris the required accreditation to fly in and compete for the Jamaican team.

Due to the unusual circumstances of the Jamaican team's four-man attempt, a record breaking 40,000 fans came to watch. For reference, the typical crowd reached about 5,000 fans. Despite their efforts, the Jamaican team did not fare too well in the races. Coming around the eighth turn on the track, the sled hit a corner, then another, and another. Running out of wall, the four-man sled crashed and soon ended up at the bottom of the track. After a minute or so, the four Jamaicans climbed their way out, smiling and waving to the crowd. Although Harris felt quite embarrassed by the result, the team quickly gained popularity by fans and even Hollywood.

This team had no background in bobsledding. They had no prior coaches in the country to introduce the sport. They did not even have the finances to do it on their own. But with the help of one man, this small group was able to make it to the biggest stage in the world. In 1944, Jamaica came in 13th place, beating several top teams like USA, Russia, Italy and Austria. Jamaica soon paved the way for more countries to do the same, including Trinidad, Puerto Rico, the Virgin Islands, Mexico, American Samoa and the Philippines.

This is the opportunity that lacrosse has right now. The sport is not yet established in many countries aside from the US and Canada, but just as Fitch did with bobsledding, lacrosse can be built from the ground up.

———

Uruguay currently has a population of about 3.4 million. To put this into perspective, the city of Los Angeles has a population of 3.9 million people. Even more crazy is that Brazil has about 3 million registered soccer players alone, almost the entire population of Uruguay! Because of this, Uruguay tends not to dominate in world affairs, in particular athletics. But one sport that the country has surprisingly succeeded is in fact soccer. Uruguay is the smallest country to have won the World Cup, with a population of about 1.5 million in 1930. The country found success partly to do with the heart that is put into the game, by both players and fans. In Uruguay, the game belongs to no particular social class, so the game has united and brought spirit to the country.

Uruguay has 15 Copas America (more than any country), two World Cups, and two Olympic titles. Although their last World Cup win was in 1950 when they defeated Brazil in Rio, Uruguay has never been an easy team to beat, and that says a lot for the size of the country. Some may attribute the success to the dynamics of their youth teams, by which many of the great players came out of and went on to play for World Cup teams.

In Montevideo, a run down stadium can be found where these great players crafted their game at a young age. It is a single field surrounded by low stands that hold around 18,000 people. There are only concrete seats, no lights, and no scoreboard. Danubio is the home club of Edinson Cavani, now at Paris-St-Germain, José María Giménez (Atlético Madrid), Cristhian Stuani (Middlesbrough), and many more. Because of the talent that has come out of the club, many consider it to be the "University of Uruguayan Football". (Independent.co)

These Uruguayan clubs are typically loaded with debt and players are often paid late or never paid at all. Still, Uruguay produces high quality talent. At these club games, there is a mix of veteran players who have come back from their European league travels, as well as young stars in the making.

Uruguay, despite it lacking in size and often lacking in resources, found a way to succeed in a very competitive sport. They showed that the top notch facilities are not necessary to start and to continue a strong program. Through their club leagues, they developed and still to this day produce talented players.

The story of Uruguay soccer is similar to the state at which many countries are with lacrosse. Some are starting to grow the game, but also feel they cannot succeed without the best resources. Although two different sports, this story shows that there is promise for a new developing country establishing this unfamiliar game of lacrosse.

With the right mix of investment, talent, coaching, and luck, one of these forty teams who have never won in lacrosse will.

———

"Dad, when did the U.S. have its first lacrosse game?" I asked.

We'd watched the opening ceremonies of the 2000 Olympic Games in Athens as a family. We marveled at the pageantry, the athletes, and the national pride. I'd been playing lacrosse (not well) for the past couple of years, and it had quickly become my favorite sport.

My parents often had to ask me not to flip the ball to myself while watching TV, eating dinner, or doing my homework. To me, it seemed obvious that lacrosse would be played in the games if they had things like swimming, equestrian, handball, and gymnastics.

"Lacrosse isn't in the Olympics," my dad said casually.

"What?" I demanded. "Wait, why not—why don't they play lacrosse? They play everything else."

My dad was at a bit of a loss.

"Maybe it's because there just aren't enough teams to have a tournament," he offered without much justification for his opinion.

I was devastated. How in the world could the sport I loved not be popular enough to be an Olympic sport? Somehow, this single revelation had rocked my young self to the core.

I'd fallen in love with lacrosse the day I picked up that stick at age four. With sisters eight and nine years older than me, I was fortunate enough to have a family who had encountered the game and could give me the resources to fall in love with it. I remember walking around the field when I was only as big as the stick, dragging it behind me because it was too heavy to lift. Still, I grew curious about how the game was played and how fast all the older kids could run and throw the ball around at extremely high speeds. I grew taller and soon was big enough to actually hold the stick in my hands without a struggle. My love for the game was growing as well, and I could not help but feel the need to share it with everyone around me. Just as my father was a coach, I felt as if I was a coach of the game even at such a young age.

I could be seen carrying a lacrosse stick around the neighborhood in my small town, eager to throw around the ball with anyone who was willing to entertain me. This often was my father, who was just thrilled that I was actually taking such a liking to sports, and in particular, lacrosse. I would come home from school and force my neighbor Drew to come over and play lacrosse with me. Drew was new to the neighborhood at the time and honestly probably thought

I was a maniac for making him come play everyday. Little did he know, he would be an influential player on our high school team.

As I grew older and continued to play the sport more and more, I appreciated more what the sport brought on and off the field. As I ran up and down the field and—in my case— stood in the goal, I felt a true purpose. This game may seem strange to outsiders who are unfamiliar with the origins and the rules, but when you step on that field, you understand.

Nearing the end of high school, I began coaching lacrosse more for my summer team. I coached players of various ages, some 3rd grade teams and some 6th grade. This ability to pass on my knowledge of lacrosse was extremely satisfying, but still, there is more that can be done.

Moving into college and developing more awareness of how society works not only in this country but in countries across the world, I soon began to imagine what it would be like for young children to pick up a stick thousands of miles away. There are countries in this world with villages unable to provide food for their families, and here I am lucky enough to run around and play this great sport.

One major detail that is crucial to the success of a lacrosse program aside from the structure is the availability of resources. For one, money is crucial to start a sport and that is especially the case for lacrosse as it is quite expensive. Unfortunately, this is not a sport such as soccer that can be played solely with a ball that can be bought for $30. For lacrosse, a shortage of money means a shortage of equipment. Without adequate resources, it is nearly impossible to find success, but with more and more programs helping with this, there is a very real opportunity there. Certain non-profit organizations, which we will go into detail in later chapters, have begun efforts to raise money in order to spread the game to countries such as Nicaragua and Costa Rica. These efforts are important to the growth of the game, especially in certain high-poverty nations, but without continued support of the game, funding can be difficult to sustain.

Of course, I love the U.S. and our commitment to and passion for the sport of lacrosse. I'll admit, I take a little bit of pride in knowing the U.S. has been one of the two nations to win every organized Lacrosse World Cup.

But I also remember that precocious kid watching the Olympics in 2000, confused as to why the sport he loved wasn't an Olympic sport.

My dad was right—"there just aren't enough teams to have a tournament."

So my goal is simple:

I want the U.S. and Canada to lose.

Not because I don't love my country, but because for lacrosse to ever truly become a world phenomenon, to become an Olympic sport of note, and to increase the quality of play for all, the U.S. and Canada must lose.

We must lose to Thailand and Russia and Australia and Argentina and Colombia.

That's right, the same Colombian team that in 2012 first established a national lacrosse program and in 2014 competed in its first Lacrosse World Games.

The same Colombian team that lost its first match 19-0 to another non-powerhouse Finland.

For the good of lacrosse, Colombia needs to be able to knock us off.

And this book is a playbook for how to do it.

CHAPTER 1

FINLAND 19
COLOMBIA 0

———

Finland just owned Colombia and was in a completely different weight class. This was the only shutout of the first games. Jarno Aaltonen had seven goals while Colombia only got off two shots.

- MARISA INGEMI,
WRITER IN LACROSSE WE TRUST,
JULY 12, 2014

July 12, 2014 was a victory for the South American nation of Colombia.

A victory? Are you sure you didn't mean to say a victory for *Finland*? How in the world could *anyone* call a 19-0 loss in a game in which a reporter said Finland "just owned" Colombia a victory?

But it was.

Just two years earlier Colombia didn't have a national Lacrosse program. The country had never before been to the World Games. And simply by suiting up a full team, competing hard and starting the process on the global stage Colombia celebrated a victory.

This victory wasn't just for Colombia—it was for all of the sport of Lacrosse.

———

Lacrosse in Colombia has made serious strides since its adoption as a national team sport in 2012—the Colombians were never expected to win the tournament (only the US and Canada ever have in its 50 plus year history). Even still, Colombia took a non-existent program and in two quick years was able to field and train a national team to play in the 2014 World Games in Denver.

To start a program from scratch and participate in the World Championships, you need to establish the infrastructure (and fast):

- Find enough Colombia-born players willing to participate and train (without pay)

- Find a coaching staff willing to recruit, train and develop a national club

- Develop administrative offices to manage logistics, sponsors, equipment

- Establish facilities for training, practice, residences

- Find clubs and countries willing to practice and compete against the team

- And find the funding to get the team TO the games

"The total cost of bringing 25 players to Denver is $64,920, however we have pooled the personal savings of all our players and have reached $40,314. Additionally, we have raised $7,840 from on the ground fundraisers."(Indiegogo.com)

The implications of playing in these World Games were far greater than one may think. By Colombia participating in the

World Games, they were able to open the eyes of so many athletes in Colombia who were not aware of the growth that the sport had already enjoyed.

In anticipation of the 2014 World Games, the government's Sports Department told Team Colombia that if they did participate in the World Games that year, they would support them in becoming an official Sports Federation within Colombia. This would be a huge lift to the growth of the sport and would mean increased funding from sports development governmental officials while allowing for the creation of paid positions for coaches, refs, and administrators.

In the end, this would allow for the creation of youth, high school, and university programs.

This would put Lacrosse on the map in Colombia.

In June of 2014, Colombia head coach Miles Makdisi named the 23 man roster that would be representing Colombia in the 2014 FIL World Lacrosse Championship in July. The roster featured players from two different clubs in Colombia: The Bogota Legends and the Pereira Wolves. Also, it featured four players who had NCAA experience with Colombia Heritage.

G - Fabian "Delfín" Ortiz - Bogota Legends
G - Ivan Florez - Pereira Wolves

D - Gustavo Rojas - Bogota Legends
D - Carlos Reyes - Bogota Legends
D - Andres Castro - Bogota Legends
D - Javier Galvez - Pereira Wolves
D - Juan "Topo" Gomez Villa - Pereira Wolves
D - Nick Fonte - University of North Carolina

M - Daniel Rodriguez - Bogota Legends
M - Camilo Lesmes - Bogota Legends
M - Gustavo Morales - Bogota Legends
M - Nicolas Garcia - Bogota Legends
M - Oscar Morales - Bogota Legends
M - Manuel Kardanass - Pereira Wolves
M - Jose Mario Valencia - Pereira Wolves
M - Will Cañas- Pereira Wolves
M - Cam Scully-Ramirez - New England College
M - Jiovany Rendon - Delaware Valley College

A - David Valencia - Bogota Legends
A - Nicolas Rodriguez - Bogota Legends
A - Julian Gomez - Pereira Wolves
A - Jesus "Chucho" Rodriguez - Pereira Wolves
A - Christian McLean - Jacksonville University

Alternates:

Diego Delgado - Bogota Legends

Fabian Barrera - Berlin HC

Sebastian "Apu" Velez - Pereira Wolves

Javier Silva - UConn Huskies/Lacrosse the Nations

Joe Prieto - Bogota Legends

———

In those games, 38 nations participated in 142 games over the 10-day period. The games began on July 10th, with a game between USA and Canada, two of the best teams in the sport.

In their first ever World Games, Colombia certainly had their struggles. In their first game, the word struggle does not even do the game justice—the reporter calling it a contest between teams of "completely different weight classes."

Playing against Finland -- another country not known to be strong in lacrosse -- Colombia fell behind early and simply was never able to shake the jitters of its first game on a national stage. With only 5 shots, Colombia was destroyed 19-0. Finland was led by 7 goals from Jardo Aaltonen and three goals by both Rick Sainthill and Roope Jokela.

But it was a start.

The team had played and competed.

Their participation in that single blowout meant Lacrosse had become an officially sanctioned sport in the Sports Federation of Colombia. The team had secured its own future.

In its next match up with some of the early jitters out of the way, the team improved—twice finding the back of the net. Their defense improved but still could not hold back Spain from scoring 14 times to take the game 14-2.

They began to improve—match after match in the tournament—trying to grow after the 19-0 thrashing they'd taken.

After their tough loss to Spain, Colombia scored 6 goals and only let in a dozen this time, losing to Mexico 12-6.

Their next game was 12-3 to Thailand. Not great, but better than they'd started.

On the sixth day of the tournament, Colombia matched up against South American soon-to-be rival Argentina and took the loss 12-3.

Their record for their first games: 0 and 6.

And yet, despite their record, it was a victory.

If you love lacrosse and have ever experienced that adrenaline rush while sprinting down the field, then you know what I know—it's an amazing sport. And this book captures what makes it great.

But what you may be surprised to learn about the sport is that it's one of the fastest growing sports in the world.

We'll talk about how it has risen in numbers so rapidly, why certain regions, programs and teams have thrived in the States, and why certain programs in other countries have already seen rapid growth.

And we'll reveal what it will take for a country like Kenya or Japan to challenge the U.S.-Canadian dominance.

Lacrosse is on the cusp of being a "mainstream sport" in America, and we'll share some of the trends that other countries will need to leverage to help it become mainstream in their countries.

Many kids grow up idolizing the greats like Michael Jordan, Larry Bird, Sidney Crosby, or Tom Brady, to name a few. These players all play or played in some of the most dominant and popular leagues in the United States or even the world. Lacrosse could someday be in that talk of the best leagues in the U.S., and young kids across the world may grow up idolizing Paul Rabil or Myles Jones, but there is some work to do before that happens. In today's world, many U.S. children are fortunate enough to grow up with the ability to play multiple sports and get the exposure to a sport like lacrosse. And there are some very well-known names out there who are outspoken or recognized for their connections to lacrosse. In fact, lacrosse was hall-of-famer Jim Brown's favorite sport.

Jim Brown grew up in Long Island, a place where lacrosse is and was very popular. In 1984, he told the New York Times that "Lacrosse is probably the best sport I ever played." A phenom of an athlete, Jim Brown was one of the most dominant running backs to play in the NFL, leading the league in rushing yards in eight of his nine pro seasons and being named an eight-time all-pro selection. In lacrosse, he was even more of a force. As a senior at Syracuse, Brown was second in the nation with 43 goals in just ten games and was named a first-team all-American. Former coach Roy Simmons told the Times that in the 1957 college all-star game, Brown "scored one goal underhanded with his right hand, one overhanded with his right, one underhanded with his left, one overhanded with his left. There was nobody like him." He was later inducted into the Lacrosse Hall of Fame. (NYTimes)

So why did this standout player not go on to become the best lacrosse player to exist at the most elite level? Well, the simple answer is that in 1957 when Jim Brown graduated from Syracuse, there was no professional lacrosse league. But if we look at this scenario in today's world, Jim Brown likely would not have been the next big thing. This is because when it comes down to it, choosing to go to the MLL instead of the NFL is insanity and would mean losing out on millions of dollars. Even today after many years of the sport existing, lacrosse is not enough for professional players to live comfortably. Most have to work other jobs because they simply do not get paid enough. In the NFL, first-year players earn a minimum of $420,000 per year. And then there's lacrosse, where rookies make $7,000! Because of this, most work jobs nearby or even in other cities, and in some cases, the MLL loses players because of full-time jobs. In order for this to change, lacrosse needs to be a recognized sport not only in the US, but across the world.

———

There's a reason international Lacrosse competitions have been dominated by the US and Canadians: it originated with the native population of the Americas.

Lacrosse began as a ritual and was embedded in native culture. The history of the sport is sometimes hard to pin down, but western accounts of the sport date back to 1637 in the journal of Jesuit missionary Jean de Brebeuf who describes entire villages playing games against one another called 'crosse'. Other historians credit the origins in the Mohawk game of Tewaaraton.

To the non-native populations it was referred to as 'stickball' and the sport was used as a means to release tension and aggression, as well as a way to settle territorial disputes. As the game grew, it became significantly more violent.

In 1870, a Creek versus Choctaw game played to determine rights over a beaver pond turned violent after the Creeks were determined the winners. As instances like this one became more frequent and culture began to diminish, government officials and missionaries began to oppose the sport. They felt lacrosse was starting to interfere with church practices and they were getting away from the origins of the game, leading to its outright ban around 1900. (uslacrosse.org)

Today, in the US, Lacrosse often receives a reputation as a sport only played by white suburban prep-school boys.

Just how did lacrosse go from a violent sport banned among the Native Americans to one of the country and world's fastest growing sports?

We have Canada to thank for that.

Lacrosse became big in Montreal and has continued to spread to this day. In the 1830s, anglophones from Montreal began to observe games and started to pick up the sport, playing with their Mohawk neighbors. The first recorded match was played in August of 1844 and by 1856 they had formed the Montreal Lacrosse Club. While the US began to ban the sport at the turn of the century, the sport continued to gain in popularity in Canada with the sport being proclaimed as the national summer sport of Canada—with the country exporting the game to England, Scotland, Wales and beyond.

A happy accident by the Canadians helped re-introduce the sport to America: hockey. Canadian hockey lovers began using their empty rinks to keep their skills sharp during the warm summer months—a tradition eventually exported to the US leading to the sports re-invigoration in the twentieth century. By the turn of the century lacrosse was becoming more popular in several countries and in 1904 and 1908 lacrosse was played in the Summer Olympics.

As of 2013, nearly 750,000 people participated in organized lacrosse with the number rapidly increasing globally. Although it has become very popular in places like the

United States and Canada, it has for the most part been very isolated to these areas. (uslacrosse.org)

————

While the sport has grown exponentially from its early days— in particular as more countries participate in international tournaments—adoption of the sport at the youth levels has remained small and slow in most countries outside of the US and Canada, which has been to blame for a big disconnect in the skill levels between these two powerhouses and the rest of the world.

Today, there are a total of 55 nations who are a member of the Federal International Lacrosse (FIL), but still no country has won the world lacrosse championship besides Canada or the US.

The FIL was established in 2008 in a merger of both the men's and women's international lacrosse associations and is the international governing body for men's and women's lacrosse. The FIL currently holds five world championships, each being held every four years. They consist of:

- Men's World Lacrosse Championship
- Men's Under-19 World Lacrosse Championship
- Men's World Indoor Lacrosse Championship

- Women's Lacrosse World Cup

- Women's Under-19 World Lacrosse Championship

The goal of the FIL is simple: For lacrosse to be played by every country worldwide and for the sport to be a recognized Olympic sport once again.

Led by president Stan Cockerton, the FIL works tirelessly to spread the game of lacrosse and establish it as a sport in every country. It does so by touching on the following areas:

1. Effective governance and financial management

2. Provide quality events and programs for our coaches, officials and players

3. Provide quality programs and resources for the International Development of Lacrosse

4. Establish and approve a set of International rules for all forms of lacrosse

5. Increase the promotion and marketing of lacrosse internationally

Since it's founding in 1972, the FIL organization has grown from just five members to nearly sixty members across six continents. In 2012, the FIL was accepted as a member of SportAccord, the umbrella organization for both Olympic and non-Olympic sports federations as well as organizers of international sports events. (Filacrosse.com)

This allows the organization to access resources and promotions, in addition to moving lacrosse one-step closer to recognition (again) as an Olympic sport.

———

The international game is not yet a *real* competition.

Want proof? The statistics say it all.

In the past 50 years, lacrosse has been dominated by only two countries. There is clearly a flaw in the way by which these non-dominant countries are approaching the sport. While you could throw blame around, the reality is that the gap has simply been too wide and no country has made the necessary investment to truly have a realistic shot at competing with the big two.

World Championship Winners:
    1967 – USA
    1974 – USA
    1978 – Canada
    1982 – USA
    1986 – USA
    1990 – USA

1994 – USA

1998 – USA

2002 – USA

2006 – Canada

2010 – USA

2014 – Canada

2018 – TBD (July)

This will change—competitive people and the growth of the sport makes it a near certainty.

But how could someone increase their chances of dethroning the Americans or Canadians?

That's what we'll dive into for the remainder of this book—but let's preview where the current gaps lie.

Want to know one of the major drivers between the top teams in any sport?

You'd probably say talent, right?

You'd be wrong.

Money.

That's right, in team sports (not individual—but this also largely applies there too) the difference between the top team performers and those that never reach the medal stand is money.

Go one level deeper. Where does the bulk of this money come from?

Advertising dollars.

Yes, when a country's fans watch a sport, advertisers follow—and for a national team to succeed, those advertisers need to fund the national team (through television and direct sponsorship).

Then all we need is more money to win, right?

Now this may not seem like a difficult task to undertake. Sure, just go put some flyers out or put an ad in the paper and people will start to hear the news. But in reality, this will not work on a large scale.

Lacrosse continues to struggle to find and retain a large audience that will catapult the sport globally—including in the markets where it dominates: the US and Canada. And if it's unable to find major advertising revenue on its home turf, it's not a wonder national programs struggle in Thailand, South Africa and Kenya.

To understand why the sport has struggled, let's dig into a few of the most successful sports and their trends in advertising and generating advertising dollars for their national programs.

Sporteology, which ranks the popularity of sports, looks at fifteen key criteria to determine global popularity:

1. Global Fanbase and Audience*
2. Viewership on TV*
3. TV Rights Deals*
4. Popularity on Internet*
5. Presence on Social Media*
6. Number of Professional Leagues in the World
7. Average Salary of Athletes in the Top Leagues
8. Sponsorship Deals*
9. Number of Countries in Which the Sport is Popular
10. Biggest Competition
11. Relevancy Throughout the Year
12. Gender Equality
13. Access to the General Public
14. Number of Amateur Players in The World

15. Prominence of the sport in sports headlines on print and electronic media*

These criterion are crucial to the success of major sports and without them, it is nearly impossible to grow.

Just why hasn't lacrosse thrived at the professional levels (or broken through as a global sports phenomenon)?

For one, the sport has seen growth in its popularity within the United States. But it's popularity has been both regional and seasonal, very rarely making national sporting news coverage. Typically high school and college lacrosse is played in the spring—but Major League Lacrosse decided to make its season over the summer (to allow new college graduates to play on low- or no-dollar contracts). While the benefits to get more top talent right out of college is a plus, summer viewership and attendance numbers are lower than spring or fall professional sporting (there's a reason baseball plays 162 games and extends into the spring and fall).

This choice of scheduling has meant a slower than hoped for fan engagement as the sport has hoped to ramp up its popularity.

This all has a trickle down effect—without a strong, popular professional league in the US, advertisers haven't 'tried out' reaching its fans, causing little to no investment in international lacrosse leagues.

For lacrosse to truly emerge on a stage to rival similar 'second tier' team sports such as cricket, rugby or water polo, a passionate fan base at the professional level will need to be cultivated (either in the US or in another country) to truly see advertisers pour necessary funds into these organizing bodies.

For international play this also matters because as a US dominant sport, the lack of advertising means less awareness of the game internationally.

———

This chapter began with the story of the 19-0 thrashing of Colombia.

Colombia is at the start of it's lacrosse program development—other countries have longer, richer histories—developing extensive youth networks to expose children to the sport at an early age. Some countries have developed programs that extend into college and beyond.

Without the infrastructure, many programs will never truly compete for a championship against the Americans or Canadians—the dominant pair of the international game.

But programs are learning and improving, making the competitions more competitive and bringing a pipeline of foreign born players into the college and professional ranks within the US and Canada.

It's these steps that have and will begin to pay off for Colombia and other countries as they look to one day dethrone the mighty two.

CHAPTER 2

MY JOURNEY TO LACROSSE

My hometown, Duxbury, MA. has been a hotbed for lacrosse in Massachusetts. There has been a huge amount of success in lacrosse in Duxbury since it started as a youth and high school sport, but in the 2000's that success peaked and at the high school level, Duxbury was dominating.

Duxbury produced extremely talented players who went on to colleges like:

- Duke (Max Quinzani)
- Georgetown (Chris Nixon)
- Yale (Reilly Naton)

- Penn State (James Burke)

- Syracuse (Hakeem Lecky)

- Johns Hopkins (Matt O'Keefe)

Growing up in Duxbury and being the slightest bit athletic almost forced me to play lacrosse.

My sisters both played lacrosse and although I clearly couldn't play girls 'lax', I learned a lot from them and in the end, did not have much of a choice in the matter - I was playing lacrosse. Both my sisters were extremely passionate about lacrosse, so when they realized I actually had an athletic bone in my body, they put a stick in my hand. Along with the help of my dad, they taught me how to play lacrosse in my backyard and the rest was history. I was on my way to becoming a lacrosse player.

Aside from my family being a huge influence on my love for lacrosse, I was very fortunate to grow up on the east coast, where lacrosse has significant popularity. For a newcomer moving to Duxbury, what was most well known was that it was a nice town on the water, there were very good academics in place, and the kids loved lacrosse.

———

I grew up about 200 yards away from the High School—an easy 5 minute walk to school in the morning if I chose to do so (I didn't). Every Sunday in the spring and summer Duxbury had a league that played at the High School called "House League". It was organized by grade and the teams were mixed up randomly. Teams were named after different colleges so there was a Duke team, a Yale team, and a Harvard team, among others.

As I grew up, my friends and I all loved playing house league because there was no real instruction on those Sundays.

We just went out and played.

One of my close friends at the time, Jack Corbett, was a year younger than me. He was a hockey and baseball player. My dad, a sports fanatic who was incredibly involved in the sports community, constantly tried to talk Jack into playing lacrosse.

Because I had been playing for so long and my dad had coached the game at different levels for a number of years, we had A LOT of spare gear hanging around our garage. One morning I had breakfast and got my jersey ready to go to the field and play. But, we took a little detour that day. My dad grabbed a bunch of extra gear, drove to the Corbett's house and told Jack to get ready because he was playing lacrosse today.

And you know what? Jack is the first to admit he still owes my father big time for that little detour we took.

After a bit of convincing, Jack gave in and jumped in the car. My dad suited him up and gave him a quick tutorial on the game. And then sent him out to the field to play with the rest of us.

Jack was a disaster. He had no idea what he was doing—sure he was decently athletic but if you've never handled a stick, don't know the rules and aren't used to the way the protective equipment feels, you're going to struggle. To make matters worse for Jack, most of us had been playing for a good two years because of the structure of our town's league.

But Jack muddled through that day. And as we dropped him off at his home he asked my father if he could borrow the stick and a ball—and hinted he'd love to play again the following week.

Jack kept playing lacrosse, eventually quit baseball and became a top-rated high school player. In fact, Jack's skill on the lacrosse field earned him a scholarship to Harvard

University—a place he admits he probably wouldn't have gotten into without his skills on the field.

As my father says whenever Jack's name comes up—"Jack was always a very smart kid but...Harvard?" It is quite impressive.

———

For lacrosse to grow globally, we'll need more kids like Jack to put down their baseball gloves, their cricket bats, their soccer balls or their tennis racquets.

The sport needs talent to truly thrive—sometimes trading a hockey stick for a lacrosse one.

Admittedly, lacrosse does have a bit of an image problem— particularly in the US. There is a bias of it being an elitist sport played by 'lax bros'—causing some people to never try it out and for the sport in general to remain under the radar for many kids.

I grew up fortunate enough to play multiple sports, including hockey. My class in school was actually immensely talented in hockey, which allowed us to play together throughout our youth.

But hockey—particularly in our part of the world—often struggles to retain top youth players as they age due to how expensive the sport is, the inability to practice outside of ice rinks, and the often complicated and fractured youth hockey structure due to the competitiveness of the sport. I was one of the lucky ones who was able to continue playing both hockey and lacrosse throughout my high school experience.

At a hockey tournament just forty minutes away from my home, I might have accidentally helped spread lacrosse to Austria.

In 7th grade, we played in a tournament in Quincy, Massachusetts that included the Austrian National team. Each year the Austrian players would stay with host families from the other teams and that year my family hosted two players, Daniel Jakubitzka and Curtis Lamp, for the week.

They were quickly indoctrinated into my family's love of lacrosse. Throughout the week, I introduced them to equipment and the sport - they were mesmerized. Daniel in particular fell in love with it, walking around our house with a stick every chance he got. They had never once seen the game played in Austria and found it to be so new and intriguing. In fact, they were surprisingly good for picking up a stick for the first time.

The sport had become so imbedded in my life back then that I did not think it was a big deal to introduce it to these

Austrian hockey players. But for them, it was a new challenge and they were eager to play.

"Here, have this," I said as I gave Daniel one of my sticks for him to take home.

He could not have been more excited. I had helped expand the sport with a simple gesture.

Talking to him in the weeks that followed, it was incredible to hear about how he was still playing with the stick in Austria.

ROADBLOCKS TO LACROSSE

For me, Jack, my sisters and all the people from Duxbury who grew up with lacrosse, we had a big advantage over people in other towns, regions or countries.

We had the equipment at our fingertips.

For Daniel and Curtis, they needed exposure, and once they had experienced lacrosse for the first time, they needed gear.

To play lacrosse, you need gear and if you don't have it—you will not likely play.

Lacrosse is one of the more expensive sports to play. In Duxbury the median household income is $140,000 and as a result my high school had a big enough budget for lacrosse that there was plenty of equipment so everyone could pick up a stick if they wanted to.

That's not the case in most places in the US—and definitely not the case outside of it.

If we are talking about expanding the game of lacrosse globally, that would not be an easy task to overcome. But, taking a step back, a comparison can be found between the costs of sports and their popularity across the globe. At the top of the list there are sports such as soccer, basketball and tennis. Each of these share one thing in common that many other sports do not: they are relatively inexpensive sports to play.

At a high level, these sports can become more expensive to play because of the quality of gear purchased for top players. But, at the beginners level, these sports can be played without major costs.

Taking youth-soccer for example, there is little that is required for kids to have adequate resources to play. Let's say a decent soccer ball costs around $50. Then, add in cleats for around $35 to $45. This is very little to get a sport started in a new country, especially if you think about the fact that a ball can be shared between a large number of kids at the youth level, and typically that is the most expensive part. This seems very attractive to someone introducing a new sport to a country and it really makes sense if you look at the statistics. Soccer has an estimated 3.5 billion fans globally and is the number one most popular sport globally.

Now taking a look at the sport of lacrosse, it's a much different situation than that of soccer. So, what really is necessary for the average or beginning lacrosse player? As a player of the sport, I have had my fair share of experiences with purchasing lacrosse equipment at every level. With the increasing popularity of the sport, equipment is being made at a higher quality so that it lasts longer than it did in the past, meaning the equipment is pricier.

Adam Ghitelman, the assistant coach for the University of Utah Men's lacrosse team and current goaltender for the Atlanta Blaze of the MLL, has had a lot of experience playing the game of lacrosse and coaching. Also a volunteer for Lacrosse The Nations, a non-profit that does a lot of work teaching lacrosse in Nicaragua among other places, Adam has dealt with the struggles as well as the promise of expanding lacrosse globally. Adam said "I also find that the barrier for entry into our sport is the biggest hurdle for most programs outside of our country. The high costs of the equipment and shipping creates financial obstacles for young programs to get sticks in the hands of their players." He has first hand dealt with these obstacles and although it is difficult to overcome, he explained how he does feel like it is a possibility.

I went with a buddy in my neighborhood, Drew, to the sporting goods store ComLax to help him pick out his gear. He'd decided to give lacrosse a try a couple of weeks back and had been using his friend's equipment. But he was already loving the game so much, so he and his parents decided it would be worth it to invest in his own gear. "Alright, let's start with a lacrosse stick, the most important part of the equipment. If you take a look at prices, you can certainly find some that can seem high." He nodded, eyes widening at not only the sheer variety of options, but the digits marked on the tags. I continued, "But realistically, a beginner does not need a stick that is any more expensive than $60. Most players tend to go for the sticks that are higher in price because they think it will make a world of a difference but it really does not for starters." I pointed to another option on the shelf, "There is no need to purchase a lacrosse head and a shaft separately at the youth level." What about the padding and all that?" Drew asked.

"Right. Then there are elbow pads, which if you find the right ones, can be purchased at around $30. Shoulder pads, also a necessity, can be purchased in the $30-$35 range." Let's go over to the cleats, uh hmm there's only a few here in store. Cleats can be a bit tougher to find but with some research, you can find some decent cleats for around $40. But they do have gloves here! A decent pair of gloves can be purchased for about $60."

"I have to warn you though, Drew, the big whammy comes with the helmets, which can be extremely expensive depending on the brand. The newest helmets are priced around $300 but this is silly for a beginner to use. For a youth player, a helmet around $150-200 should do the trick, but I know that is still a big bill to pay."

So, all together you are looking at about $370-$425 worth of equipment for one beginning player. Quite expensive!

This is a tough obstacle to overcome, especially for players and programs trying to get started at the youth level. Without some sort of outside source of funding or donors, it is going to be an expensive sport for a parent to put their kid in.

However, consider the overall cost of lacrosse at a competitive level when compared to those other sports like soccer, football, basketball, and baseball.

A	Lacrosse	Soccer	Football	Basketball	Baseball
Headgear (Helmets)	200	-	200	-	20
Shoulder Pads (and elbow)	30	-	100	-	-
Cleats	40	40	40	-	40
Stick/Bat	60	-	-	-	50
Glove(s)	60	-	-	-	65
Ball(s)	20	30	30	20	30
Other	-	*20	**80	***150	-
Total Cost	410	90	450	170	205

* Cost of soccer shin guards

** Cost of additional football protective gear (thigh pads, hip pads, pants, etc.)

*** Cost of a basketball hoop

As you can see, the costs of playing lacrosse are still fairly high due to the amount of equipment needed compared to other sports such as soccer and basketball. Still, football has lacrosse beat on the total cost and football is still a tremendously popular sport. In the United States especially, football has become one of the most watched sports and people worldwide have become fans. So, the costs, although high, have not stopped the sport from taking off.

In addition to the great subsidies and scholarships many clubs and even schools can offer to players for whom equipment and other costs can represent a financial burden, in comparison with these other athletics, the cost of lacrosse can seem overwhelming. But, with the right amount of research and forethought, there are ways to get around this obstacle.

Now, let's talk about actually playing the sport. In the United States, most kids usually join a club team which acts as their youth program growing up. Club programs can vary in cost depending on its prestige among other things. According to the Baltimore Sun, you can find club teams to join in Maryland for around $700 a year or some can even cost more than $1,600 a year. This includes uniform and tournament fees as well as club expenses, such as coaches' salaries and facilities.

With the popularity of the sport growing in the US, program fees are only going up. Laxachusetts, a successful club program I grew up playing with in Massachusetts, also follows this trend. Players are starting earlier and playing more often. Costs vary depending on the amount of playing you want to do. For example, for middle school kids to play 6 consecutive Sundays during the winter, the cost is $350 per player. Although this is costly, the club does do a great deal to better each and every kid involved.

Hong Kong is currently in the midst of expanding lacrosse to a large audience. The Hong Kong Lacrosse Association, the governing body of lacrosse in Hong Kong, was founded in 1993 and is a member of the Federation of International Lacrosse (FIL), Asia Pacific Lacrosse Union (APLU), as well as Sports Federation and Olympic Committee Hong Kong, China (SF&OC). The Hong Kong Lacrosse Association (HKLA) has announced plans for the Men's Field Team to represent Hong Kong at the 2017 Asia Pacific Championships June 16-24, 2017 in Korea, and at the FIL Men's World Lacrosse Championship in 2018. 2018 will be the Men's 5th World Championship, having represented Hong Kong in the 2002, 2006, 2010 and 2014 World Championships.

"The sport may be little-known to many in the city, but with the backing of a wealthy patron, has big plans to expand its popularity and success". In Cantonese, lacrosse is translated as "Stick net ball", and tennis is "net ball". Quite understandably, many people get confused by the difference and do not even realize "lacrosse exists". "If I clarify, most people can't picture what it is – so they usually just smile and say, 'Good luck'!", said Carrie Hui Ka-hei, captain of Hong Kong's women's lacrosse team.

In Hong Kong, lacrosse has been played at universities and that has made advertising the sport much easier. Universities can provide a very reliable and expansive platform that makes awareness easier. In order for the sport to grow and be a community game, the common assumptions and misconceptions must be torn down. "My mission is to develop and promote the sport to the general community – there's a perception that it's a minority 'elite' game and that's just not true," said Raymond Fong Kun-sheng, chief executive of the Hong Kong Lacrosse Association (scmp.com).

In Sporteology's list of key requirements in identifying the top sports across the world, one was access to the general public. Because lacrosse has been seen as a luxurious sport and strictly for the elite, many do not feel the need or ability to try to play. For Jay Wich, a former Harvard University student and one of the leading scorers during his time playing at Harvard, he had to make the decision between lacrosse and finance. Because lacrosse in its current state does not pay the bills, Wich chose finance. On top of this, Wich was moving to Hong Kong where he thought it would be unlikely that he would ever pick up his stick again. Within 6 months of arriving in Hong Kong in 2007, Wich found himself again with a stick in his hands. He started his own team in a local league and before he knew it, was representing Hong Kong in the World Games. (scmp.com)

With the help of a private benefactor, the team has been able to travel to tournaments, including the recent World Championships in Denver. The team had a full sporting staff, including sports psychologists and five trainers, and finished as the second best Asian team behind a Japanese team. Although he thought his lacrosse career would end upon graduating from Harvard, Jay Wich is happily playing the sport he has grown to love and is helping grow the sport he loves at an international level.

As a current lacrosse player who has been through many years of the game (youth, high school, college), I have seen the good and bad in the ways that lacrosse has been advertised to the general public. From seeing Austrian kids pick up a stick and fall in love with the game to a friend of mine being somewhat forced to play and eventually finding himself playing at Harvard University, there is a lot of good to come out of the sport and time can only tell what the future will hold. As I traveled to Denver my junior year of college with Georgetown University to play against the Denver Pioneers, I got a sense as to how the game is truly being noticed. For one, it is very impressive to see how the Denver team has enjoyed such success in an area that is not traditionally a hotbed for lacrosse. As we arrived to the airport following our game in which we lost pretty handedly, I decided to take a walk and get some food. I found a small sandwich shop and after ordering,

I waited for my food to be called. All of my teammates and I wore suits for the trip, a new dress code implemented by our coaches. Two women standing next to me who were also waiting for food asked me where I was from and what we were doing here, noticing all of us in suits. I explained to her that we were traveling back to DC and that we had just played a lacrosse game at the University of Denver. In response, the women said "Oh! We know lacrosse" and explained how they were from Texas but have noticed how much the sport was growing out there. In fact, one woman's son was playing in high school. Even though I was not in the best of moods after Denver's face-off star Trevor Baptiste single-handedly won the game, I could not help but smile. It showed a lot that these two people traveling back home to Texas, where lacrosse certainly is not a priority, noticed not only what the game is, but how much it is growing.

INSIGHTS FOR GROWING A NATIONAL LACROSSE PROGRAM

- Present opportunities for youth to play early on through rec leagues and tournaments.
- Share the game as much as possible, even to friends and family.

- Do not be overwhelmed by the cost of the game. Much of the gear can be of lower quality for a first time player. The only cost that will seem high is the helmet. If you are introducing lacrosse to kids who have no idea what the sport is, start with only a stick and lacrosse balls: The rest of the gear can be purchased at a later date.

- Start off with low-costing gear - That will be more than sufficient to grow the game. Both STX and Nike offer sticks for beginners that are relatively cheap. Warrior and STX both also offer protective gear, some at very high prices, but others for beginners that come at a low cost. Shoot for these to start.

CHAPTER 3

FACILITATING YOUTH LEAGUES

—

With the growing exposure worldwide, there are many efforts to introduce the sport to new countries, from Jay Wich's experiences in Hong Kong, to Kids Lacrosse The World in Africa and Lacrosse The Nations in Nicaragua. With this comes a lot of responsibility and there is a lot that must be put in place in order for a program to be successful. It was discussed how youth programs have been implemented in other countries, but to better understand this structure and the "ideal" model, we should understand what we have here in the United States in addition to the efforts being made outside of the country.

Dan Chouinard, Sean Morris, Dave Evans, and Mike Connelly are co-owners of the Laxachusetts Program that is rated as the best in New England and also a top-five program in the US. The club offers participation for each grade level through high school as well as a developing program for young players K-3rd who are trying to develop lacrosse skills. With over 85 coaches on the staff, Laxachusetts has an abundance of knowledge to offer. They have 3 US Lacrosse coaches of the year, 14 coaches with professional, college or international coaching experience, 1 former MLL commissioner, and 20+ league/state coaches of the year. In addition to this, many of these coaches have had a great amount of success as players. Every coach has played college lacrosse, 15 were College All Americans, 25 High School All Americans, 3 NCAA National Champions, 15 coaches with professional playing experience, 4 Team USA players, and 10 MLL All-Star selections. The credentials are certainly there! Laxachusetts has had over 419 players to go play at the college level.

So why focus so much on what Laxachusetts has done? Sure, I come from this program which could be a reason behind all of this, but it is what the program stands for and how they develop players that makes them stand out.

"There was a lot of "lax bro" going around and not much lacrosse instruction and there was ZERO focus on personal accountability. A lot has changed in the past 10 years on the Massachusetts lacrosse landscape. We are encouraged by some of the efforts by other groups to better instruct their athletes and even mandate SOME better behavior."(Laxachusetts)

Lacrosse can certainly get a bad rap, from both those who know the game and those who have only heard of it. Laxachusetts focuses on developing the character of the player and not just the on field skills. I remember coming in for one of our first practices of the year when I was in 7th grade. At that age, we all were a little bit "on our high horse", thinking we were the best thing ever. But that first day, the coaches, led by one of my favorite coaches in the game, Mike Connelly, explained how we would be different. We were not going to be lax bros. We would respect the game and act accordingly. That included no flat brim hats. As silly as it sounds, little things like that is what made the program successful. Absolutely, I wore a flat brim a few times outside of lacrosse, but I sure as hell didn't show up to Laxachusetts practice with one of those hats on. It was all about discipline.

Laxachusetts' program also made an effort to develop their players in the off-season. That was a huge part of the success of the program. That didn't mean having practice every day in the winter, but there were winter sessions as well as guides for players to put in the work on their own. Even to this day that is followed. I remember this past fall my younger cousin, who is a freshman in high school now, was going crazy because Laxachusetts was doing a "Wall Ball Challenge" where kids had to post a video in which they had to do an assortment of passes without any mistakes, including behind the back passes. Those who succeeded were given a new customized Laxachusetts helmet.

On the field, coaches practice different drills they have learned in their time playing. Such things consist of ground ball drills, footwork drills and cradling. A particularly fun game the coaches came up with is called "Steal The Bacon". A ball is placed at the midfield line and players are divided into two teams. Each team spreads out along opposing lines about 25 yards away from the ball. Each player is given a number and the numbers on one team are also equal to those on the other. The coach calls a number and the two players who have those numbers sprint for the ball in the center. The player who picks up the ball then have to cradle and cross his own line to score a point. In addition to competitive games like these, players are taught proper shooting skills and practice hand eye coordination.

Although Laxachusetts puts a lot of emphasis on discipline and fundamentals, the program also stresses creativity.

Laxachusetts offers an indoor box lacrosse league for players to take part in if they wish. Box lacrosse is a tool that is being used more and more. Players are becoming more skilled today than in the past and it is almost crucial to develop stick skills, which box lacrosse certainly helps with. If you think about some of the best players to play at the collegiate level, most if not all have incredibly strong stick skills. Think Lyle and Miles Thompson. Both have exceptional stick skills and both played box lacrosse growing up. Two of the biggest names in the sport. That is not to say by playing box lacrosse you will be the next Tewaaraton winner, but it sure does not hurt!

Crabs Lacrosse is another program that has dominated the lacrosse scene since its start and its reputation has only heightened. They started as 1 team in the summer of 1990 out of Baltimore, Maryland. This was really the start of summer club lacrosse for the Crabs and what started the dynasty of a program. Now, the Crabs have experienced years of success, fielding only 1 team per graduation year in order to bring in the best players around.

Over time, the Crabs have been able to thrive partly to do with the outstanding coaching they receive. Many are coaches at some of the top high schools in Maryland including DeMatha Catholic, Boys' Latin, and Loyola Blakefield.

Andy Hilgartner is currently the Head Coach at McDonogh School in Maryland. He was named the Midwest Coach of the Year in 1997 and the Maryland State Lacrosse Coaches Association Coach of the Year in 2010. He also coached in the US Lacrosse Champion All-American game in 2011. Coach Hilgartner's teams have won 189 games in his 15 years as a Head Varsity Coach. Ben Rubeor currently serves as the head coach at Loyola Blakefield. In the last 3 seasons he's led his team to 3 straight MIAA Final Fours, including an MIAA A Conference Championship in 2015, which earned him the USA Today National Coach of the Year. He graduated from Loyola Blakefield in 2004 and won the C. Markland Kelly Award as the best player in Maryland that year. He went on the University of Virginia, where he was a 3x All-American, 2x Tewaarton Finalist, 2x Captain, and played on the undefeated, 2006 NCAA National Championship team. After graduating from UVA, he played for the Chesapeake Bayhawks for 8 seasons, captained the team, won 3 MLL Championships, and finished as the Bayhawks' all-time leading scorer. The Crabs put a lot of focus on lacrosse IQ, much of that coming from the many knowledgeable coaches they have gained over the years.

At the high school level, the goal for summer lacrosse is to get recruited to play in college. The Crabs have certainly managed to provide the platform for high school players to gain exposure, and it has shown through the number of players they have sent to college teams. They have sent players on to schools such as North Carolina, Harvard, Maryland, Princeton, Virginia, Johns Hopkins, and Duke among others. A few big names who went through the Crabs program are Conor Doyle (Notre Dame), Wells Stanwick (Johns Hopkins), Deemer Class (Duke), and Brian Phipps (Maryland).

Crabs is a Maryland 501-C-3 Non Profit. Players pay between $1250 - $2000 depending on the team for the summer season. This fee includes:

- Tournament Fees
- Uniforms
- Equipment
- Facility Rental
- Practice Time
- Site Insurance
- Coaching Stipends
- Administrative Costs

Because of the competitive nature of the program, the Crabs hold tryouts every year, which means that players are not given a spot on the team just because they were on the team the previous year. This aspect, along with other parts of the Crabs program have driven them to a lot of success.

The Crabs are a part of the National Lacrosse Federation, in addition to Team 91 NY, Long Island Express, Leading Edge, HHH Big 4, and Laxachusetts. This enables them to compete in the most elite of tournaments, enabling their teams to compete against the best of the best. The Crabs have also partnered with Nike, another testament to the reputation of the program.

———

Lacrosse is not an easy sport to introduce in a new place. But if you can introduce it early—the possibilities are endless.

Outside of pure advertising dollars, one of the single best ways to grow a sports talent base is through youth leagues and programs. One of the biggest issues with growing the sport is the large amount of funding that has to go into it. Because funding is a major issue for many countries trying to start the sport, many non-profit organizations have begun efforts to start lacrosse.

For example, Kids Lacrosse The World is a non-profit that has done exactly this and deals with the struggles to fund staff, equipment, and other costs. "This amazing non-profit has been supplied and operated exclusively by donations and partnerships."

Kids Lacrosse The World focuses on promoting leadership and empowerment at the youth level through the sport of lacrosse. This non-profit works in small communities in Kenya and Malaysia Borneo to develop and create sustainable student centered programs to develop their youth. As lacrosse has begun to reach an international scale, Kids Lacrosse The World has strictly focused on spreading the game at the youth level.

The program started through volunteer trips and has continued to make strides towards growing lacrosse in these areas since. It has received help from local fundraisers, school equipment drives, among other funding efforts.

"Together we achieve more" is a phrase that can be useful to many and has been for Kids Lacrosse the World. With the help of companies such as Lacrosse Unlimited, Viva Lacrosse, JIMA LAX, Un1tus and many others, this non-profit has been able to open up the game of lacrosse to many who haven't had the opportunities to play before, all the while creating a better place and life for these youth.

With its unique focus solely on developing the youth, the foundation certainly focuses on bettering the person and uses the game of lacrosse as a medium to help lives.

Elliot Couch, the founder of Kids Lacrosse The World, took a trip back in September of 2016. He traveled, along with Samson Tan from NYC, to Ranau Malaysia. There they built the first youth lacrosse program in Southeast Asia. Each day, the two spent about 4-6 hours with students of the SMK Mat Salleh, a local public school. Over 12 days, the pair taught over 200 kids, developing their passion for lacrosse, all the while enriching their English and teaching them life skills.

"By the end of the 12 days, students and educators mentioned to me how they've never seen the students work together and be so excited about something new."(Couch)

Although nobody had even heard of lacrosse prior to its introduction in Ranau, you could now go to the local public school and see young kids throwing the ball around on the field.

For Elliot, the decision of whether or not to travel that far to start a program was not an easy one. There were a lot of factors that went into the decision and whether his efforts would actually create a breakthrough for the sport there.

For one, the idea to travel Malaysia came after an English teacher, Kelly Case, constantly contacted Elliot explaining how she wanted to introduce a new sport to the community. The idea sounded great, but how reliable could this be? They had to deal with the fact that they had minimal sponsors and partners, and would be traveling 40 hours during flights and another 3 hours by car to just reach this community.

With the help of Samson Tan, who had started inner city programs, the two started a program involving clinics and practices centered around the kids' class time. Reaching more than 200 players, the program focuses on 2-3 hour sessions every day with 35-40 students age 15-18. In addition to the coaching, KLTW donated 2 lacrosse goals, 26 girls/boys lacrosse sticks and 32 lacrosse balls. The donations were sourced locally in Denver and donated by numerous youth lacrosse clubs, associations and high school teams.

For newcomers like these kids, lacrosse is a fascinating game, but it is not only the sport itself that keeps so many players involved. "A student came up to me and thanked me, not for bringing lacrosse to her home town, but for providing the chance for her to make new friends and enjoy herself while being with others all through a new sport." (Couch)

For SMK Mat Salleh, there is a lot that must be done and many obstacles to overcome in order to further grow the sport. For one, difficult issues such as wildfires, earthquakes and other events out of their hands can hinder the growth of local programs. Also, for the game to grow, school officials must get involved so that schools can connect students to the new game.

———

"All right here we go!" Ryan exclaimed.

I started the engine, and we started roaring our way through Nairobi. Patiently, we drove through the day and night and before we knew it, we were on our way to the Butula Hekima Academy to start a youth lacrosse program in Kenya, Africa.

After a successful trip to Malaysia, the program set out to Africa to set up their next lacrosse program. In a more jungle-like area, the program set forth building goals, the first step in their expedition. Immediately a large group of students from the school surrounded, wondering what in the world was going on, as Elliot and others hammered nails into wood to build their goals. After much hard work, they had two 6x6 lacrosse goals ready for play.

The next morning, Elliot, along with Ryan Rabidou of Inside lacrosse and coworker Danielle, set up their four session lacrosse schedule for the students.

- Session 1: 9-9:40 a.m.
- Session 2: 10:20 – 11 a.m.
- Session 3: 12-12:40 p.m.
- Session 4: 3:30 - 4:30 p.m.

"9:05 a.m. nobody out here, 9:10 a.m. still nobody, we just stood around with big grins and jumpy feet. Suddenly, about 30 students run for their lives out onto the field yelling and screaming, it was Class 3, 8 to 9-year-olds."

With practice jerseys donated by Un1tus in Ohio, lacrosse sticks donated by Lacrosse Unlimited in New York, and balls from SlingItLacrosse in San Francisco, the first session was a success.

Eager to learn but very confused at first, Elliot and Ryan showed the young group how to properly catch and throw. Surprisingly fast learners, they went on to teach them how to cradle before they had to get back to class.

In the last session of the day, the oldest of the kids were taught in a more fast pace, moving from catching and throwing to

2 on 1 ground balls, shooting drills, and "games of steal the bacon, which we dubbed "steal the sugar" considering the local area is known in Kenya for its sugar plantations."

As the week went on, they noticed that a growing number of kids were coming to play and were eager to learn more about the sport. It was expected that there would be a fairly large group that would become interested in the sport and develop a passion to continue playing.

In Butula, Kenya, the only similar sport in the area was soccer, in which the kids were using a deflated ball and no goals. But, since the program got started there, around 400 students have been introduced to lacrosse and 30-40 have been playing regularly. The school has 20 girls sticks and 20 men's sticks, as well as only about 45 lacrosse balls to supply the entire program. The resources are limited but the heart to play the game is certainly there.

In the predominantly Muslim region of Malaysia Borneo, a program was set up in the town of Renau, within two schools. Elliot and other volunteers have helped teach lacrosse to around 400 students here and around 80-90 are playing the game regularly. With only 45 girls sticks and 35 guys sticks, the supplies are low and is not even sufficient enough for all of their regular players.

For these young kids, lacrosse has become a source of hope. It gives them an escape from their everyday life, where the bar to succeed is not set extremely high.

Kids lacrosse the world has been supplied entirely by donations and partnerships. Elliot Couch works as a special education teacher in Denver and has received generous donations from the Denver area. Thanks to donations from the likes of lacrosse unlimited and others, some organizations are making strides to improving funding efforts.

———

Lacrosse The Nations is another non-profit that has taken major strides in expanding the game and changing the lives of youth kids. Started by Brett Hughes and Brad Corrigan after a conversation in 2008, the two decided to use lacrosse as a vehicle to improve the lives of those in need across the world. Brett is a former All-American, Team USA and MLL player from the University of Virginia. He played 6 years in the MLL. Brad is a musician with the internationally renowned band, Dispatch, and played lacrosse at Middlebury College. The goal is to teach their students valuable life skills and health education. LTN has a meal program, academic support, and a life skill curriculum that they have implemented in their time serving these communities. So far the non-profit has been able to set up programs in Nicaragua, Costa Rica, and

Charlottesville, and from talking with both Brett Hughes as well as Javier Silva who is the Executive Director of LTN, it is obvious their efforts are going to continue to impact a larger audience.

LTN's main focus is not on the success of these kids as lacrosse players but rather developing them as people. The game of lacrosse and sports in general help develop players as people and allow them to learn a lot about life through the game. This includes being able to work with others, work ethic, motivation, discipline, and confidence just to name a few. "The curriculum serves to teach life skills through lacrosse as well as a series of games, team building activities, challenges and reflection—consciously intertwining the playing field with the daily routines of the children who participate in our programs." On the lacrosse side, practices are offered before and after school to children ages 8-21. The practices are organized into three sections:

1. Introducing a lesson - the coaches and directors will introduce a new lesson that practice for instance, goal setting. They will then discuss its importance and how students can go about reaching their goals.

2. Use lacrosse to reinforce lesson - the coaches take the field with players and go over things such as

shooting techniques and drills associated with that specific lesson.

3. Reflection - The whole group will come together and talk about what they liked out of the lesson, what they learned, and how they could change it to make the lesson better. Usually lessons will be reinforced over multiple classes.

In addition to this, the curriculum is organized into four units, each with 9 classes:

Unit 1 – Taking Care of Ourselves and Each Other
Unit 2 – Teamwork and Cooperation
Unit 3 – Respect and Sportsmanship
Unit 4 – Health

———

Lacrosse the Nations has three international programs. Two in Managua, Nicaragua and one in Playa Potrero, Costa Rica. A program is also in Charlottesville, Virginia. As it continues to grow, the success of LTN is not always measured because the impact of improving the lives of these kids is really immeasurable.

- Club Hope: 40+ students ages 10 and over through before and after school lacrosse programs

- Chiquilistagua: 800+ students in grades 2-11 through in-school PE and after school lacrosse

- Playa Potrero/Brasilito: 80+ students of all ages, per quarterly sessions, through after-school lacrosse program

- Charlottesville, Virginia: 40+ summer campers, and 30+ summer league participants

LTN works both with kids in school and also with kids outside school. Lacrosse is offered both as an in-school PE program as well as an after school program. LTN invites kids who are not enrolled in school to participate in the after school program and through that, LTN tries to encourage their enrollment in school. With all that LTN does, it certainly is not all smooth sailing. "Funding is somewhat difficult in all NPOs. You have to attract and engage a donorship and our programs are not down the street. They are in Central America and that sometimes can make it hard for people who don't really understand the incredible amount of work we are doing as it's not something they can see whenever they like." (Brett Hughes)

It has always been the goal to implement a lacrosse team in the places they travel to, but as was mentioned, it is not the first priority. "Our goal to bring a Nicaraguan lacrosse team has been 9 years in the making. We needed to first get involved in the community and create real meaningful relationships and help out the communities with their basic needs before we could do anything else."

Since the organization's start in 2008, it has made major strides and plans to expand its programs in Nicaragua. In addition to this, LTN is working to build a U-19 team to take to the world games. This program has done great things in its time spreading the game of lacrosse, but it is not really about spreading the game of lacrosse. Certain countries, such as those that LTN work with, do not need the sport right away. There are many other resources they need but lacrosse acts as a springboard for these other necessities to happen.

———

On a more local level, Harlem Lacrosse is a program that has made tremendous strides at spreading the game of lacrosse to kids who are not fortunate enough to have the ability to otherwise play the sport. "Harlem Lacrosse's mission is to empower the children who are most at risk for academic decline and dropout to rise above their challenges and reach their full potential. Harlem Lacrosse inspires children to dream about tomorrow while working hard on the field and in the classroom today." Similar to the other organizations we discussed, Harlem Lacrosse places a strong emphasis on bettering the individuals they work with as people and students as well as lacrosse players.

Harlem Lacrosse brings in special education students and students identified by school administrators as vulnerable to academic decline or dropout. This means that they are serving high poverty students that most organizations or normal lacrosse programs would not aim to teach. In fact, 96% of Harlem Lacrosse students are qualified for free or reduced lunch.

Harlem Lacrosse realizes that the goal in every young players mind is to make it to the college level. So, the program teaches these kids the perseverance, grit, and confidence that they need to make it to that level in the classroom and on the field.

It was in 2008 that Harlem Lacrosse Co-Founder Simon Cataldo joined the faculty of Frederick Douglass Academy I (FDA) in Harlem as a Special Education math teacher with Teach for America. He ran into many struggles in his first year which is why he introduced lacrosse as a way to engage these particularly challenged students. With just 10 sticks for

11 students, Simon took to the field and by the end of the year, was astounded at what he found. Simon's players posted the highest scores on the state math test by Special Education students in FDA's history.

In 2011, after growing to 35 players, Harlem Lacrosse was formed to create a holistic youth services organization in hope that these kids would achieve more in the classroom after finding success on the field. Since 2012, Harlem Lacrosse has added at least one program each year and now operates eleven programs in New York, Baltimore and Boston serving over 450 boys and girls at FDA, P.S. 149 the Sojourner Truth School, P.S. 76 A. Philip Randolph, Promise Academy II, and the Commodore John Rodgers School. The program is even planning to launch in Philadelphia in 2017.

Harlem Lacrosse program directors are not there to serve just lacrosse but also act as tutors and mentors. This comes through many activities, character building instruction, and also daily study hall.

Harlem Lacrosse students have maintained a 100% on-time middle school graduation rate, have passed their classes at a rate 20% higher than that of their peers at their school sites, and have earned over $15 million scholarship offers to independent schools and colleges since 2012. It is quite remarkable how just a small program that did not even have enough sticks for each student ended up being such an important part of hundreds of kids' lives. Through this, Harlem Lacrosse students have earned access to several schools including Bates College, Colby College, Connecticut College, Gettysburg College, Haverford College, Hobart College, Tufts University, the University of Virginia, and the U.S. Military Academy at West Point.

Much of Harlem Lacrosse's success can be attributed to the amount of effort and passion put forth by all those involved in the program. After talking to Spencer Riehl, a Senior Program Director in New York, I was extremely impressed by the dedication he had towards bettering these kids' lives through lacrosse. It is clear that Harlem Lacrosse will only continue to grow and impact more lives with the use of this amazing sport.

INSIGHTS FOR GROWING A NATIONAL LACROSSE PROGRAM

- Encourage personal as well as skills development
- Look for non-profits already working to help establish youth lacrosse in your nation

- Start young: Offer a diverse age range for kids to play

- Develop a plan: What is the goal of your program? What type of culture do you want to instill?

- Compete: Provide games for the players to showcase their development

- Have fun: Lacrosse should be a fun sport. Even if you are creating a program to win games, players need to have fun in order to appreciate the sport.

CHAPTER 4

LIVING LIFE AS A
LACROSSE PLAYER

———

Playing lacrosse at the highest level is a dream many kids who pick up a stick are eager to achieve. But how tough is it actually to reach this goal? We hear about the many great players like Paul Rabil, Casey Powell, and Lyle Thompson and how their lives have revolved around the sport. But these players are very rare cases. For most, the game of lacrosse is a long journey, in some cases ending up at the highest level in college, but others taking paths much different. This chapter will give an insight into the journeys of a few lacrosse players who have ended up at different levels of the game but who have all made it their mission to continue to grow as a lacrosse player. With this, we can develop an understanding as to how someone in a country new to the sport could also make lacrosse a big part of their life, even from a young age.

THE MLL CHAMP

Growing up in East Meadow, NY, Tom Schreiber has played lacrosse for as long as he remembers. He officially started playing when he was in 3rd grade, but as far as he is concerned, there was a lacrosse stick in his crib. Schreiber had uncles who played lacrosse and a father who played, all who were extremely influential in his career as he grew older.

"I played for my town PAL program from 3rd to 6th grade – The East Meadow Jets. We played other towns in Nassau County. From there, I played for Long Island Metro and then the Long Island Express. These were travel teams where we played 3-5 tournaments per summer," he explained.

Schreiber had a unique youth lacrosse experience because his dad was coaching all the way through. His dad was very knowledgeable in the game and demanded a lot of the players, constantly trying to improve them. And this only carried through high school.

Ever since he was little, Schreiber knew he wanted to play lacrosse in college. As Schreiber put it, "Growing up, NCAA

Championship Weekend was our family vacation." And this dream of playing at the highest level could not be stopped. His goal was simple. He wanted to attend a division 1 school that also was a top notch academic institution. This goal landed him at Princeton University.

Per Ivy League rules, the team was only allowed to practice with their coaches 10 times. So, throughout the fall and winter they lifted, conditioned, and had practices held by the captains. The spring was when the time commitment ramped up. They practiced Monday to Friday from 4:30-7:30pm and lifted twice during the week before morning class.

After a successful career at Princeton, Schreiber went on to dominate in the MLL, winning the championship with the Ohio Machine in 2017. Despite having a large amount of success in college and the major league, he explained how he simply enjoys being a part of the team and the bond they share.

The game of lacrosse has certainly given him a lot on the field, but it has also done a great deal for him off the field as well. In college, Schreiber's team traveled to Costa Rica, where they ran a few clinics and scrimmaged the Costa Rica National Team. After this experience, Schreiber went on a trip to Uganda, which really opened up his eyes to the world. He explained how passionate the players were about the sport and stated how "to this day, I get questions about improving." In 2014, Schreiber was even able to coach the Uganda National Team in their first ever World Games experience.

When asked about his thoughts on the future of the game, Schreiber stressed how he hopes it can become a global sport. He said how "it is a game that anyone can play regardless of size. Athleticism helps, but you can make up for it with superior stick work."

THE LONG ISLAND PHENOM

Born in Long Island, New York, Dan Bucaro, now an attackman for the Georgetown Hoyas, was introduced to the sport of lacrosse at the age of 4. Because of the prevalence of the sport in his area, his life revolved around lacrosse from an extremely young age and has brought him much success throughout his life.

"Two gym teachers are credited with bringing lacrosse to Long Island from New York City in the 1930's. After World War II, the city all but forgot about the sport, but on Long Island the suburban population was exploding in the 1960's and lacrosse boomed with it."(NY Times)

Being introduced to the sport by his dad, who is a sports fanatic himself, it was the programs he grew up playing in that really developed his passion for the sport.

Dan played for Three Village, a youth program out of Setauket New York and as he explained, it was a fairly competitive program for a young kid. The program was just kids from his town, but because of the sport's popularity, Three Village was able to play in leagues against other towns and even travel for tournaments. From the ages of 5-13, Dan would practice around 3 days a week, each year increasing his skills and love for the game.

This program provided a lot of structure and enabled Dan to make an easy transition into high school, where he only saw his game rise to a whole new level. A four-year letter winner for lacrosse and a captain of his varsity team his junior and senior years, Dan was a two time all-American and a three time all-county selection during his career. He helped lead Ward Melville to a national championship during his sophomore season, scoring 57 goals and tallying 30 assists for the year.

As it grew quite obvious Dan's talent was at a very high level, he became determined to continue the sport at the collegiate level. Drawn by the team, coaches, and reputation of the school, Dan decided to attend Georgetown University where he has only continued to grow as a person and a player. As a teammate of Dan's at Georgetown, I can fully attest that he has the skills and the heart to be one of the best in the game. Dan literally eats, sleeps, and lives lacrosse. I cannot count the number of times he has told me he wants to start a lacrosse company with me, which I can certainly see happening in the future.

The amount of exposure to lacrosse that Dan received at a young age was extremely influential in his success as a high school and college lacrosse player. From playing in tournaments with Three Village to stepping on the field for Ward Melville, the structured programs paved the way for Dan to continue to grow.

THE WHEAR BROTHERS

Just as it had for Dan Bucaro, lacrosse has been a gateway for both Matt and Scott Whear, natives of Duxbury, Massachusetts. Duxbury has been a hotbed for lacrosse and has given life to many star players including Max Quinzani (Duke and MLL) and Chris Nixon (Georgetown and MLL).

As brothers, Matt and Scott grew up playing every sport together including football, hockey and of course, lacrosse.

At the age of 7, they were encouraged by their father, Gary, a lifelong athlete and star hockey goalie at Babson College, to try lacrosse.

Duxbury has a very competitive youth program, and even at a young age, leagues were structured to create as much playing time as possible for newcomers. Playing as much as 4 times per week, kids would gear up after school or even play under the lights on the turf field. In the spring, Duxbury youth practice would be held nearly every day.

"We played almost everyday in the spring. We would travel to CT and Long Island to play other valued programs, and other deep-rooted programs," Scott explained.

Because the Whears and their teammates played so frequently, their team was dominant around Massachusetts. This forced them to travel elsewhere to find competition that would be at a higher level than they had been playing. When they traveled to Connecticut, they often played Darien, a team that soon became a major rival for Duxbury.

Because of how much opportunity it gave its young players to participate, the Duxbury youth program has developed highly skilled players who have continued on to higher levels.

Scott Whear continued on to play at the collegiate level at Wheaton College, while his brother Matt went the military route to attend Norwich University.

THE WEST COAST KID

Stephen MacLeod grew up in Marin County, California, an area not really known for playing lacrosse. He was introduced to the sport in 5th grade at the age of 11 or 12 and never turned back. Like many other young kids, Stephen started off playing baseball. After one of his friends began playing lacrosse, Stephen decided to make the switch away from baseball, which he felt was too slow paced and really didn't enjoy.

Because lacrosse had been mostly dominated by east coast programs, California was much slower to be exposed to the sport. For Stephen, his early days of playing lacrosse would certainly face its ups and downs. He played for the Southern Marin Wolfpack, a generally well run local program. They had games once a week on Saturdays or Sundays and the competition was decent considering the state's slow pace to take on the sport. But when he reached 7th grade, the program essentially dropped off. That year, they only had enough kids to field a B team and often had to practice on tennis courts because the fields were constantly damaged by rain and other conditions.

In 8th grade, Stephen switched over to the Ross Valley Grizzlies, a program run with much better coaches and far more organized than his previous program. In transitioning to high school, Stephen noticed the much higher intensity and pace of the game even stating, "If I had stayed in the Wolfpack I would have been far behind. Overall there was a lot more pressure in high school lacrosse that didn't exist in youth programs." Stephen definitely felt the pressure as he grew up. He has some memories, not all good ones, that shaped him as a person and as a lacrosse player. "I got shit on a lot by the coaches for forgetting my pinnie and shorts." The accountability was far more noticeable in high school than it had been before, despite his year with the Grizzlies.

Later in his high school career, Stephen began to notice that this game could be a springboard for him to get a good education. He knew that he wanted to play at the division 1 level and was determined to do so upon realizing his lacrosse abilities were good enough to allow him to compete at that level. He decided on Georgetown University, a school notable for its academics and prime location. Lacrosse can open up so many doors that couldn't have been opened before and that was also the case for Stephen. "It also helped me get into

Georgetown which would not have been possible otherwise," he explained. The ability to leverage a sport to further your education is a very powerful tool, and all the while playing a sport you love is pretty remarkable.

Although it can be a very difficult jump to make, the transition from high school to college went pretty well for Stephen, a big strong player who made his mark as a young defenseman for the Hoyas. After a lot of hard work, Stephen started to play a large amount of minutes for the Hoyas, noting one of his favorite moments coming when he got to guard Austin French, who he played against in high school, in the Hoyas' game vs. Denver.

THE "STAG"

Now a "Stag", Matt Sharpe grew up with a strong program to help define his game as a lacrosse player. Growing up in Duxbury, Massachusetts, lacrosse is the talk of the town in the spring, as the high school team has brought home 9 state championships in the last 15 years. But it hadn't always been that way. Until the 2000s, Duxbury had not been as dominant as they have come to be and because of that, players didn't always get the credit or respect that they deserved. But as the Dragons began to win state championship after state championship and the more talented players began to move on the division 1 level, the town became known for its lacrosse. Guys like Max Quinzani, who went on to be a star at Duke, and Chris Nixon, who went on to be a strong player at Georgetown, gave the program a lot of credit that it needed to cement itself as a powerhouse for Massachusetts.

It all starts with the youth programs. Duxbury's youth programs have always been strong because of the amount of involvement from coaches who really knew what they were doing. "All the coaches were great and always harped on practicing on our time and being the best that we can." The involvement was incredible and as Matt pointed out, the coaches really stressed the extra work necessary to compete at a high level. If you ask any player about their youth careers, most if not all will point out a particular coach that made a major impact on their growth as a player. For Matt, this coach was Gib Brady, one of his first coaches as a young player in Duxbury. "He was the first coach to really take me under his wing and tell me about all the potential that I had. He believed in me since day one and always knew I would be able to achieve my dream of playing Division 1 college lacrosse," Matt explained.

But as Matt reached high school, the difference in play was quite noticeable. The amount of talent the program already had was incredible, and coming in as a freshman in high school was a scary thought. Most (if they were smart) players did not try out for the varsity team unless they truly had a chance of making it. Matt's freshman year, only one freshman made the varsity team. Matt spent that year on the freshman team, but it was an extremely important year that helped prep him to play a big role on the team in his sophomore season.

Matt even remembers his first varsity goal at Duxbury, and a pretty important one it was. It was against Medfield, an in state rival of Duxbury. It was a tight game and although it was only his first year as a contributor for the team, Matt stepped up and scored a crucial goal to help beat Medfield. "It was a tight game and I caught the ball on the crease and scored a backhand goal. I was incredibly pumped to contribute in such a way in such a big game."

For many youth and high school kids, Division 1 lacrosse became a dream because of its increasing prevalence in the US. Since he started watching it on ESPNU as a young kid, Matt knew he someday wanted to be at that level and playing on the big screen. So, as his high school career progressed, he began to get the attention of many D1 schools, one of those being his future school, Fairfield University.

Like it had been from youth to high school, the transition from high school to college was not an easy one on the field for Matt. Once reaching the division 1 level, you know that you are playing with the best of the best, and that is exactly what Matt found from his first day on campus. His first year was a learning experience as it is for most, so he remained on scout team for the duration of the year. After a lot of hard work, Matt was able to earn himself a starting position as a midfielder in the first 5 games of his sophomore season, before getting injured. Although injury took him out too early, Matt has grown as a player and the effort sure has not been lacking.

The time commitment is crazy at the division 1 level. In the fall, the Stags practice Monday-Friday from 7-9am, with workouts mixed in 2-3 times per week. In the spring, they practice Monday-Friday from 11-2. Film is held every day in the spring, either before practice or sometimes as early as 7am. In addition to that, spring workouts are held on Mondays and Thursdays after practice. The only time away from the game and school is the day or two they get to go home for Easter break.

The commitment is very real at this level, but has Matt explained, they all knew what they were getting into before they got there.

THE VIRGINIA/HOLLAND/ENGLAND/PITTSBURGH NATIVE

Tucker Gillman grew up in various different places such as Virginia, Holland, England, and Pittsburgh. They all vary greatly in the competitiveness in athletics, but in 4th grade, Tucker started playing lacrosse and never turned back. Because of his like for the physicality of the sport and the fact that his friends also played, Tucker got involved in the local youth program. Every spring they would have a team organized and played in one summer tournament. The team was coached by a few of their dads with knowledge of the game or even knowledge of sports in general.

As Tucker got older, there was involvement in the youth program from former college lacrosse players and that definitely boosted his passion for the game. "My brother never got the same level of coaching so he never grew to like it as much," Tucker explained.

Coach Kielbasa was one of the guys who gave Tucker the love for the sport that he needed to reach the next level. He was a former Army lacrosse player and brought a tremendous amount of energy. Although he was a pretty intense guy, coach Kielbasa taught Tucker to have fun with the sport, while also teaching him the necessary skills along the way.

Always a hardworking kid (I can attest being his teammate now), Tucker did not find the transition from youth to high school too difficult. Playing youth, he was always taught to put in the extra work and make the extra effort to get better. But, Tucker did find that his lacrosse IQ needed some work at the high school level.

Tucker certainly had what it took to be a great lacrosse goalie. His presence on the field (and off) was unlike most players and he really knew how to communicate which is very necessary to be a goalie at the highest level. So, in deciding where to go to college, Tucker knew he had to play at the D1 level. There was no way he could play D3 because he knew that someday he would have regrets. Because of the reputation of the school academically as well as athletically, Tucker decided to attend Georgetown University.

What he realized upon arriving to campus on September 1st, 2015 was that the skill level and athleticism of every player was much higher than at the high school level, so it took some time to adjust.

Tucker's love for lacrosse has been aided by some great coaches and teammates in his time playing, but it hasn't always been a smooth ride. He has hit some bumpy roads with teams struggling to find wins and dealing with the life of a college lacrosse player. Still, this sport has brought him become so much success on and off the field and has made him a better person through it all.

KEY TAKEAWAYS:

- Pick up a stick early: It is never too early to start playing lacrosse.

- Structure is key: Find a youth program in order to have a schedule of practices and games.

- Don't be afraid to fail: Lacrosse can bring with it a lot of opportunity but it is not an easy sport.

- Shoot for the stars: In reality, you want to shoot for the back of the net, but when it comes to setting goals, aim high. Strive to reach the highest level, whether that be high school, college, or even professional.

- These experiences and takeaways can certainly be implemented in other countries as well. It is through the failures that we will soon find success, especially in the case of lacrosse.

CHAPTER 5

THE IMG EXPERIENCE

Growing up in Ithaca, NY, Massi Bucci started playing at just 5 years old. He grew up in an area where lacrosse was fairly prevalent, so the opportunities to play were all right there in front of him. He had the resources and access to the sport which is an obstacle for others.

"I really enjoyed the people and the sport itself. Also as I grew up I always dreamed about playing in college," Massi said. Massi explained how he grew up in a well established youth program that really helped groom him as a lacrosse player. Many of his coaches were crucial in growing his interest in the sport.

When Massi reached high school, it was the programs that he grew up playing in that helped make it a fairly easy transition.

For Massi, it was a quick decision that he would continue on at the collegiate level. He had the skills and dedication to play at a high level, which helped him when he decided to play Division 1 at Georgetown University. Combining great academics with high level competition, the decision seemed simple.

Before attending Georgetown, Massi made the difficult decision to leave his local high school to attend the IMG Academy. IMG Academy is a private school designed to develop the highest level of play in each and every athlete that attends in addition to seeing each player carry a full high school academic workload. For Massi, this meant putting in a lot of hours into lacrosse in preparation to play at Georgetown. The program combines indoor box field skills as well as outdoor development and competition. This technique, known as DoubleCrosse, is designed to develop a skills based foundation to enable the athletes to play at a high speed with high level level skills. The programs successes have been obvious: ranked top-10 nationally in both 2015 and 2016, and developing 25 division 1 athletes since 2013.

You would think that IMG would be located in one of the hotbeds of lacrosse, but it is actually located in Florida, a state not known for its lacrosse talent. In US Lacrosse's 2015 participation report, 305,122 high school kids participated in lacrosse in the United States, a 2.7% growth from the previous year. From this number, there were 176,039 male players and 129,083 female players. Lacrosse is currently the fastest growing sport and this certainly shows at the high school level as well. In 2015, 2,677 schools sponsored the sport.

Within the high school demographic, there are definitely schools that have had a dominant history and places that are "hotbeds" for lacrosse. When most people think of the hotbeds of lacrosse, they typically think of Long Island and Baltimore, among a few others. But, as the sport grows, the sport has been reaching more states and developed high-level talent across the country.

Region	Number of Players	% of DI Men's Lacrosse
Long Island (NY)	386	13.90%
New Jersey	277	10%
DC Metro Area	175	6.30%
Massachusetts	144	5.20%
Upstate/Central (NY)	138	5%
Canada	127	4.60%

Region	Number of Players	% of DI Men's Lacrosse
Philadelphia/Main Line (PA)	126	4.50%
Fairfield County (CT)	110	4%
Baltimore Metro Area (MD)	102	3.70%
Ohio	76	2.70%
Westchester County (NY)	75	2.70%
Anne Arundel County (MD)	73	2.60%
California	64	2.30%
Colorado	56	2%

The growth of the sport at the high school level is creating less dominance in just one region across the country. There are many states that have not gotten publicity related to lacrosse, Florida being one of them. Although the state does not have nearly as many participants as dominant states such as New York, Maryland and Massachusetts to name a few, Florida's growth rate in the sport is huge. From 2009-2013, Florida experienced a 70% growth in the number of lacrosse players, just second to Minnesota (73%).

But one school that has had no troubles getting in the spotlight recently is IMG Academy. A boarding school and sport training venue in Bradenton, Florida, IMG has about 1,000 students enrolled at the high-school level. But, this is not the normal high school that the average kid grows up attending. IMG focuses on its athletics and is proud to develop their student-athletes into the best versions of themselves. This does not mean all who attend IMG decide to go on to play college sports, but the numbers are definitely significant. In recent years, the lacrosse program has improved drastically, getting major respect nationally and producing talent to compete at the collegiate level.

- Top-10 national rankings in 2015 and 2016
- Three All-Americans since 2015
- 25 D-I commitments since 2013

But how did this boarding school become so dominant? Florida surely hasn't produced the best talent in recent years because of the state's recent introduction to the sport, but at this point in time, IMG is a school very capable of playing and beating schools in the hotbeds of lacrosse.

Is it the facilities? Well, it is undeniable that these facilities are state of the art and these student athletes are being treated like professionals at the high school level. Lacrosse players at IMG have access to 20+ multi-purpose fields, a 40-foot lacrosse wall for skill development, 65,000 square-foot Performance Center with a 12,000 square-foot weight room and a covered turf facility. If that doesn't sound attractive, I don't know what does. Still, the amazing facilities cannot account for all of the school's high success.

As the nation's only full time lacrosse residency program, IMG offers a lot that normal schools cannot. "Our program aims to develop the complete player by integrating indoor (box) and field lacrosse through individual instruction and team building. Our student-athletes graduate with the technical skills, game-level IQ, and the strategic awareness that is so essential to succeeding at the next level."

Focusing not just on development on the field, IMG develops it's athletes off the field as well. This means physical conditioning, athletic body management, nutrition, vision training, mental conditioning, leadership training, life lessons, as well as college prep.

Within their physical conditioning program, IMG's team of experts designs a program based on the sport and necessities of the athlete, assuring they will reach their highest potential physically. This comes through training in speed and agility, endurance, strength and balance, and even flexibility. Assuring they have the best coaches to develop their athletes, this is also accounted for in the weight room.

The current strength and conditioning coach, Matt Wheaton, was a former lacrosse player and coach who has had an exceptional career before landing at IMG. His experiences included head strength coach of boys and girls' lacrosse, boys and girls' soccer, and alpine skiing at Yarmouth High School. Matt was also the head coach of the Junior Varsity girls' soccer team and Junior Varsity boys' lacrosse team at Yarmouth High School, while also working as a strength and conditioning coach at Beyond Strength, a private facility focusing on athletic development and sport performance in high school and college athletes. In addition to this, Matt is a Sport Performance Coach for USA Weightlifting. Similar to the approach at the college level, IMG helps athletes manage their bodies while they perform in their sport. This comes through athletic training along with physical therapy, regeneration massage, sports therapy, and education on injury management.

Nutrition also plays a major role in the life of an athlete at IMG Academy. For most high school athletes, this is not really a resource most have access to or even something they would think about. In my days in high school, I never even thought about the effects of eating a healthy diet. But at IMG, student athletes are educated on:

- Optimal Everyday
- Nutrition
- Athlete Eating Plans
- Nutrient Intake and Timing
- Hydration Strategies
- Dietary Supplements
- Body Composition and Framework
- Body Weight Issues
- Energy Balance

A more unique style of training that IMG uses is vision training. Since quick reactions and good eye sight are necessities in athletics, especially lacrosse, IMG helps train the eyes of its athletes through eye muscle and visual system exercises. Vision training enhances:

- Hand-eye coordination
- Peripheral vision
- Reaction time
- Depth perception
- Vision Strength

Another area that is not typically highly focused on but is crucial to the success of all athletes, especially at the next level, is mental strength. IMG's Mental Conditioning Program helps athletes produce a highly productive mental mindset in order to build confidence and determination necessary for athletes to reach their potential. It helps develop:

- Mental Toughness
- Awareness
- Energy Management
- Thought Management
- Teamwork

The next major focus of the IMG program is that of leadership development. With all their fancy equipment and top of the line facilities, it would be easy for student-athletes to become caught up in the perks. But at IMG they have put a particular emphasis on developing the athletes into better people along with their skills on the field. What really stands out about the school is how much concern they have for the person as a whole and not just as an athlete. The typical high school lacrosse team will practice after school and there is little other training outside of this set schedule, besides maybe a weight room lift here and there. But at IMG, the goal is to develop leaders through communication skills, conversation skills, accountability, and character building among other things.

- The goal:
- Effective Communication
- Authentic Leadership
- Media Training
- The Power of Collaboration
- Interview Skills
- Building Team Culture
- Developing Identity

The final two pieces of the IMG experience comes through college planning and life skills training. Of course, college planning can be an extremely stressful process and for a high school student, there is a lot that is unknown about the process.

- Helps with:
- College Planning
- Application Education/Assistance
- Athletic Recruiting
- PSAT, SAT and ACT Prep

- NCAA Compliance Education

- Alumni Network and Support

With the number of student athletes going on to attend highly competitive colleges, it shows that their training certainly pays off. IMG tries to help student-athletes to get the full experience while they attend the school. They try to help students along the way, but at the same time want students to become independent and be able to function on their own.

Student-athletes will develop

- Personal Growth

- Responsibility

- Peer-to-Peer Interactions

- Health and Wellness

- Career Planning

- Adaptability

- Organization and Time Management

"I owe much of my success to the innovative education and training programs at IMG Academy. My three years at IMG contributed significantly to my development as a student, athlete, lacrosse player, and as a person. I felt unbelievably prepared when I walked on campus as a Freshman and earned a starting position on the team."- Ben French Member, Team Canada U-19 National Team; starting attackman, University of Vermont

IMG has developed a great number of lacrosse players who have gone on to attend highly prestigious universities. To name just a few, IMG has sent lacrosse players to Harvard, Dartmouth, Virginia, Michigan, McGill, Syracuse, Albany, Marquette, and Georgetown.

Massi Bucci is currently a freshman at Georgetown University and former IMG Academy lacrosse player. Since leaving IMG in 2016, Massi has had a lot of success on the Hilltop. After a solid fall performance, Massi was named as a first line starting midfielder for the Hoyas. Unfortunately he was injured just a few games into the season, but Massi has gotten a taste of what the future could hold for him at Georgetown.

Much of this success can be attributed to his time at IMG and his growth as a person and athlete. Massi did not know much about the boarding school before a friend of his had brought up the idea. Talking with an old college friend during a reunion back in Massi's hometown of Ithaca, NY, Massi's dad Gary Bucci mentioned that Massi was looking for boarding schools to attend the next year. Coincidentally, this friend was actually the director of lacrosse at IMG and recommended Massi go take a visit.

"I chose to go there because when I got there, I was blown away by the facilities and I felt there was no other boarding school I had toured that would give me an experience I needed to succeed. Another unique thing was that it was in Florida and I could play year round," he said. Upon arriving at IMG for his first year, Massi was definitely not disappointed by the facilities or his experiences.

In regards to being a student at IMG, life was similar to how it is in college, with around 3 classes a day that last about an hour and a half each. "Similar to college it was block scheduling so on Mondays and Wednesdays I would have 3 hour and a half classes and on Tuesdays and Thursdays I would have 3 different classes. Fridays would alternate classes. School would end at 1230 and at 2 the devotion to athletics would begin. In the fall the weeks would consist of field lacrosse Monday, Wednesday, Friday and box lacrosse Tuesday and Thursday."

The winter was more devoted to lifting weights and cross sport training so we would lift Monday, Wednesday, Friday play lacrosse Monday-Wednesday then play basketball or football on Thursday and have Fridays off. In the spring it was

Field lacrosse Monday-Friday." In the fall, they conditioned before practice and lifted after practice.

As far as the work that was necessary outside of the field, as was discussed, IMG dedicated a lot of time to bettering their athletes as a whole. They would have nutrition classes once a week for 4 weeks in the fall and the nutritionist was always available outside of those required times. Massi said that "in the fall there were many classes we would take in the afternoon that focused on different things. Leadership was one of those classes in which they provided techniques to help manage situations. The school was interested in developing the athlete as a whole both physically and mentally. So along with leadership classes we had vision classes, mental toughness classes, and yoga."

Although they put a significant amount of emphasis into playing sports, the IMG staff knew these were still high school kids they were dealing with. "We still had a lot of free time because we really only had about 4 hours of our day devoted to lacrosse, which is similar to college, so if a kid wanted to play in college but didn't like that, it wasn't the right thing for him."

Aside from the structure of the IMG program, the staff also played a major role in the success of the student athletes.

There were two full time coaches that ran the two teams at IMG. Massi explained how they were always available, which made his experience a lot smoother. All of them were former lacrosse players so they knew what it was like to play the game and be in his shoes.

Massi's assistant coach at IMG was Jason Basso. Massi explained how he had a tremendous impact on his growth as a player and a person during his three years at IMG. "We were very close and I could tell him anything so I think that personal connection I had with him obviously built the coaching bond. By my third year there I was also in a strong leadership role so I was an extension of the coaches so I would give him a trustworthy players viewpoint on how things were going." The results certainly show that the structure and foundation of IMG Academy has lead to a lot of success. And sure, those million dollar facilities aren't a bad touch.

The program that IMG has been able to construct is quite remarkable and would be a very high expectation for most to reach. But let us think: Is this concept possible to build in other areas like Florida that are not popular in the sport? How about other countries?

Sure, it would not be an easy task to take on. You would need funding, and a lot of it. But aside from the funding put into IMG, the concepts and goals the school sets for each student-athlete can be done elsewhere. The school invests in great coaches, ones who are also great teachers. Similar to the way many of these non-profits that were discussed in early chapters did, IMG focuses on bettering the person as well as the player. They put an emphasis on the well-being of the athlete mentally and physically, as well as their growth in the classroom. This is important not only for developing a player, but also for developing a successful program as a whole. This organized plan set up by IMG has a purpose and is how they have produced so many outstanding student-athletes.

KEY TAKEAWAYS:

- Develop the full person and athlete: skills only can take a player so far. It is absolutely necessary to develop players mentally in addition to physically.

- Sport focused: for new countries eager to find success in athletics, the IMG model is a path that makes a lot of sense. It allows kids to grow as students while placing an extra emphasis on their sport of choice.

- Top programs can rise in non dominant regions: Florida is not a hotbed for lacrosse but IMG became one of the top programs in the country. It is about what happens in the confines of the program itself that define a team.

CHAPTER 6

REALITY CHECK

——

Graduating from high school is a great time in a young person's life and you look ahead and imagine an ideal college experience. Most students are ready to move on from the stresses of high school and the confines of nagging parents and all sorts of other things that seem to fill their days and take away any free time. But what they don't realize is...college is hard. Very hard. You are now living on your own and have a whole lot of freedom...to make mistakes... and if you don't fix those, it can be a roller coaster of a ride.

Now, add in playing a Division 1 sport, let alone a college sport in general, and your life is going to turn in to the ultimate test. For a young student athlete, arriving to college in the fall is an exciting time. You get to see your coaches, who seem like the nicest people on earth, on campus for the first time and you get to meet the guys who will likely be your best friends for the four years you are on campus and in many cases for life. You move into your dorm and set up your room with your parents helping you make it look presentable, despite the fact it will probably look like a dump two weeks later. The next day your parents leave and you are left to conquer the world of college.

This is awesome! You can hang out with friends, go to parties, and do all the other things that college student do. And you're a college athlete so people will think you're cool, of course. Well, no, that's not really what happens. Sadly, everything isn't how it's portrayed in the movies. Instead, you are preparing for a run test that is a week later and you are not the most gifted runner ever and it's not going to be easy. From experience, the run test is not a fun ordeal. And as a goalie, I came in thinking it wouldn't be the biggest deal in the world if I didn't pass the run test. Wrong again!

Let's run through a typical run test at Georgetown University:

> I found there was a strong emphasis on hard work from the day I stepped on campus. This run test was not just a test of how conditioned we were physically, but it was also a test of how mentally strong we were.

This was a whole new ball game from high school. I no longer just had the job of sitting in the goal and stopping shots. We were required to run as a team and work as a team. We were going to be a strong unit, which was why the run test was an important step in that process.

** Note - the run test requires you to pass all 10 runs**

RUN TIME REST

1 Lap 70 s 60 s

120 19 s 38 s

120 19 s 90 s

17 60 s 90 s

300 (50 yd) 60 s 90 s

17 62 s 90 s

120 21 s 42 s

120 21 s 90 s

300 (75 yd) 62 s 120 s

4 Stop 2 minutes END

DESCRIPTIONS:

1 lap – One lap around the entire football field (including the endzone).

120 – Start at football goal line. Sprint to far 40 yd line and return.

300 (50 yard interval) – Start at the football goal line. Sprint to 50 yard line and back 3 consecutive times.

17 – Start at football goal line. Sprint 15 yds, stop, and turn around. You will sprint 15 yds 17 times.

300 (75 yard interval) – Start at the football goal line. Sprint to the far 25 yard line and back 2 consecutive times.

4 Stop – Start at the football goal line. Sprint to the far football goal line and back. Sprint to far 25-yard line and back. Sprint to the 50-yard line and back. Sprint to near 25-yard line and back. (Similar to a suicide)

For some, this may make no sense at all, but let me tell you is it hard. So in week one, you prepare for the worst run you have experienced in your life. The fall is a bit more laid back than it is in season because there are restrictions on the number of hours you can play. What this really means is you are expected to play a lot more on your own. And you spend a lot of time off the field working on strength and conditioning. Including lots of running!

Then classes start. It's pretty overwhelming the amount of work you have and the little free time there is to handle it all.

The typical schedule for the fall can be rough, something I know from experience.

Monday: 5:30am wake up. My roommates and I stress at the fact that in thirty minutes we will be running stairs. 7:00am lift. After lift I go to classes, which are usually an hour and a half each. Some days I would have one morning class and others I would have two. After lunch, I would go to individuals, which were essentially practices by position group. So, as a goalie, I would get individual instruction for about an hour with the other goalies. Then, once individuals were over, I would eat real fast and head to my last class of the day.

Tuesday: 7:30am study hall. After study hall, I would go to breakfast at the dining hall with my teammates and then go to my first class of the day. Again, class lasted about an hour and a half. Following afternoon class, I would go eat dinner and at around 8pm would need to go to the library to study.

Wednesday: Same as Monday
Thursday: Same as Tuesday
Friday: Same as Monday and Wednesday

Unfortunately, life as a college athlete is not all fun and games. You cannot just walk onto the field and casually throw the ball around like it is a summer league. The level of play at the college level is significantly tougher than that in high school and significantly more intense than high school. The high school days were, for the most part, laid back and stress free. But when you step on that field in college, you have a job. Your job is to win games and you must do everything necessary to prepare for each and every game. That means waking up at 5:30am on Mondays and sprinting up the Exorcist stairs (if you haven't seen the movie, look it up).

Now, as stressful and brutal as I just made college lacrosse seem, it is also the best hard work you will ever experience. It is the perfect example of what you put into it is what you get out of it. College lacrosse teaches you the power of hard work, how to deal with adversity, and even how to grow as a leader.

My freshman year of college was a big eye opener in many ways. The fall was a tough experience, something that I had not experienced ever before. The running was far more extreme than I imagined and the early wake-ups were not easy. After the fall, we kept pushing. I found my groove and began to feel more comfortable on the field and had started to prove myself as a starter for the team. This certainly helped me push through the brutality of the winter, which was filled with conditioning, more conditioning, and then even more conditioning. Despite my love for conditioning (that's a joke, that's why I play goalie), there were times that I would feel I couldn't push through any longer. But it was the help from teammates that pushed me that extra yard.

Those extra yards proved to help significantly as we moved into the spring. We had all the talent and the leadership needed to have a successful team. Despite that the beginning of the season did not start off successfully and if we had not stuck together as a unit, we easily could have fell into a losing season.

Confidence was a major part of our success as a program my freshman year. We were by no means cocky, but we always remained confident in our abilities as players and as a team. In addition to this, we had captains and senior leaders who kept us in this positive mindset throughout the season. That leadership is extremely important for a team and a program to be successful.

The first game of the year was against Notre Dame, a powerhouse in Division 1 lacrosse. It would be a huge mountain to climb but we were certainly up for the task. On top of this, it was my first career game and I was starting in the goal. I am a very calm and collected person and when it comes to lacrosse, I rarely get nervous. But it was impossible not to be nervous for that first game.

Days before the game, my teammates expressed to me how confident they felt in my abilities and me being "the guy" in the net for the opening game. The game ended 14-12 Notre Dame, our first loss of the season. Although we played a very solid game, a loss was a loss.

The next game was our home opener against a strong Towson team. We came out very slow that game and the Tigers took a 6-0 lead. Wow! I could not believe what was happening. We just played the #1 team in the country in Notre Dame, losing by only two goals but now we were losing by 6. The final score of the game was 9-6 Towson. Despite losing the game, it showed the potential we had as a team. After going down 6 goals, we held Towson to just 3 more goals and were able to cut the deficit to 3. But, we had a lot of work to do.

After the Towson loss, we regrouped as a team and had a long talk about our goals as a team.

1. Win the next game
2. Make the Big East
3. Make the NCAA Tournament

After a brutally tough but excellent week of practice, we won the next game and the next three after that. We stood 4-2 going into a game against Duke, a team that has consistently been at the top of the rankings. The stands at Georgetown that Saturday afternoon were packed with people, rooting on both the Hoyas and the Blue Devils. We again showed a lot of signs of excellence but made too many little mistakes to win the game. The final score was 15-13 Duke, our 3rd loss of the year. Although we were disappointed about the loss, we did know one thing: we were no average team.

The next game was against Loyola, a team who had built themselves up to be a talented group with a good reputation in the lacrosse world. With a recent national championship under their belt, it was certainly a team we could not take lightly. So we prepared that week as we would any other, but had a little chip on our shoulder after such a close game against Duke. I remember that Wednesday night game against Loyola vividly. There were not a ton of fans in the stands that night but the environment seemed electric, part of that having to do with the energy coming from our bench.

It was late in the fourth quarter and we were tied 12-12 in a hard fought battle by both teams. But I can still remember feeling this confidence in myself and in my teammates that night. I knew for some reason or another that we were not going to lose that game. We scored late in the quarter on a goal from senior Bo Stafford and after a face-off win in the last minute, held onto the ball to secure the win.

"So, what was it that made this team so special", I began to think. I have thought about this question for two years and still do not have the full answer. What I do know is that we had the seniors that showed the rest of the team how we were going to handle ourselves, on and off the field.

Leadership: one of the most important parts of a team, whether that be in a business, a study group, an organization, or an athletic team. If you have strong leaders at the top who can lay a strong foundation for the rest of the team to follow, the chances of success are much higher. This is certainly what I experienced in my freshman year at Georgetown. From day one on campus, the seniors made it clear that we were going to be a good team, but that it would not be an easy task.

Within this senior class were different leaders who behaved in different ways. Regardless of whether they had a "C" on their jersey or not, they all still behaved like leaders on and off the field. Because of this, every person on our team respected them, especially the freshmen. They were an intimidating group, but when it came down to it, we knew they would have our backs. I vividly remember one of the seniors, Bill, who from day one we knew was not someone we wanted to mess with. He was a big, strong kid who carried himself with confidence. For the first month or so, the freshman did not really form much of a bond with Bill because quite honestly, we were afraid of him. But, after a few months we earned his respect and he took us under his wing and made an effort to develop a relationship with each and every one of us.

One key ingredient that all good teams have, in my experience playing lacrosse, is very strong relationships between teammates that becomes the driving force for the team's success. There have been teams with enough talent to win championships but for some reason, they just cannot win the big games. It is the factors aside from skill that break these teams, whether they were lacking leaders or they did not have a strong team bond.

That season, we went 10-6, a huge improvement from the previous year. We ended up making it to the Big East Conference finals and lost to the Denver Pioneers, who went on to become the national champions. Although the year did not end with a trophy, it gave us a small taste of what it is like to compete on a good team and the work, on and off the field, which is absolutely necessary to succeed.

Before my freshman year, the Georgetown Lacrosse team had a record of 4-10. My freshman season, in what was supposed to be a rebuilding year, we took a talented group of players combined with tremendous leadership and team chemistry to put together a strong season. This is not an impossible thing for a new program to do. In the future, lacrosse should be a world-wide sport. And with that growth will come the opportunity for there to be lacrosse programs at the university level. And those programs will have the opportunity to become successful in a short period of time if all the necessary ingredients are there.

In 2014, The University of Richmond launched their Division 1 Men's Lacrosse program. They lost 7 of their first games 8 and ended the season 6-11. Just one year later, Richmond would have a winning record, finishing 11-5. In 2017, the team finished 12-3, just three years after launching the program. This is a team comprised of a lot of solid players, but none that were supposed to be the best in Division 1. Still, they were able to be one of the top teams in the country.

It is absolutely possible for a new college program to find success early. Some of that success will come after experience and with some failures along the way, but with a strong foundation and adequate leadership, the possibilities are endless.

TAKEAWAYS:

- What you put into it is what you get out of it: nothing good comes easy and that certainly applies to lacrosse. Strong teams have their fair share of struggles but through these they grow and find success.

- Leadership is key: there will be many talented programs. The championship caliber teams have great leaders - ones who will develop strong bonds with teammates but who will also push their teammates to the extreme. Leaders can come in many different forms and leadership does not have to be dictated by a "C" on a jersey.

- Finding success early is possible: just because a program is new does not mean it has to fail. Richmond is the perfect example of this - after one bad year the team went on to be one of the top lacrosse teams in the nation.

CHAPTER 7

THE COLLEGE DREAM

Soooo… You're a pretty talented lacrosse player in high school and "the ceiling is the roof" as Michael Jordan would put it. You are deciding on college and you know you want lacrosse to be a part of your life. You have two options: you go big and play D1 or even D2 or D3, or you take your talents to the club lacrosse route and enjoy the college experience without the pressure or structure of the higher levels of lacrosse.

What most don't realize is how many steps that are necessary for a college to even add a sport in the United States. Adding a sport to a college or university is not an easy thing to do and there are definitely many requirements and obstacles. For a university in the United States to add a college sport, they have to adhere to the title IX rule which states that there must be equal opportunity for both men and women student athletes. This can become a major problem for some schools who hope to add a male sport but not the same women's sport.

According to Title IX of Education Amendments Act of 1972, the federal law states that "No person in the United States shall, on the basis of sex, be excluded from participation in, be denied the benefits of, or be subjected to discrimination under any education program or activity receiving Federal financial assistance."

This law applies to both public and private institutions that receive federal funds.

Essentially, this law means that

1. Women and men must be provided equitable opportunities to participate in sports.

2. Female and male student-athletes receive athletic scholarships proportional to their participation

3. Equal benefits for male and females: ex. Equipment and supplies, scheduling games, travel allowance, tutoring, coaches, facilities, housing, etc.

There are some caveats to this because the fact that there must be equal opportunities for both men and women does not necessarily mean it must be in the same sport. Men and women are fully able to play different sports, so under title IX, there are separate requirements for certain situations. For example, for the equality in regards to equipment, football gear will certainly produce a much higher cost than for example women's soccer because of the amount of gear needed in football. So, as long as the gear is adequate in both sports, in this case football and women's soccer, there is no violation in title IX, despite the equipment budget being much greater for the football team.

Just recently, St. Bonaventure University in Allegany, New York, announced that it will be adding men's lacrosse for the 2019 season. Currently operating with a successful club lacrosse team, this will be the 17th division 1 sport at St. Bonaventure and they are expecting around 45-50 student-athletes to be added for the program.

St. Bonaventure's did previously have men's lacrosse at the Division III level from 1989-93 but then was changed to a club sport, where it has remained until now.

With this addition, St. Bonaventure would become the 72nd Men's Division 1 program and 13th program added in the last decade.

"Lacrosse is one of the fastest-growing sports in the United States, and it is already one of the most popular sports in Canada. We have a successful club team and significant interest in adding the sport at the varsity level as well. Also, the men's program will complement our women's lacrosse program well and give us another sport that I believe can be very competitive. For all these reasons, we are excited to add men's lacrosse."

"The sport of men's lacrosse has shown tremendous growth in recent years. Total participation rose 95 percent from 2000-2014 with the number of teams across all NCAA divisions. That continues a trend of great expansion for the sport as whole – 57 teams were announced to begin in men's and women's lacrosse during the 2016, 2017 and 2018 seasons. In all, 71 institutions currently sponsor Division I men's lacrosse."(gobonnies.sbu.edu)

The next step for the university is to hire a coach and find a conference to join.

So, what exactly are the qualities and necessities of an excellent college coach?

First, we must understand that being a college coach is not an easy job by any means. Your job is to win games and doing that alone is not a guarantee that you'll be judged as a success. You also have to deal with young student athletes who are learning who they are as people and often making many mistakes along the way. Your job is almost always in the public's eye and every little mistake made by your players falls back on you. Whether it's fair or not, people judge coaches: fans, parents, the media, and even your own team. It is not for everyone.

Most of the time, coaches are judged solely on their record. You win games and people love you. But, if you lose games, your job may be on the line. It's the reality of sports and coaching. Some great coaches in college are great because of the talent on their roster. They may not actually be a tremendously skilled coach but are great recruiters, but because they win games, it may look that way. On the other hand, there are some very skilled coaches who are tremendous teachers of the game, but don't have the talent to have a great team (rare).

But there are certainly qualities necessary to run a successful team and to develop the talent on that team to the fullest. The coaches who can develop their players and help them grow will find success one way or another. But what really makes a GREAT coach great?

1. They make their players believe in themselves:
    All players in college already have a degree of
    talent that's helped them reach that level, but
    for them to reach greatness, these high-level
    coaches inspire and motivate them to find that
    1% more. These coaches are able to spot when
    their players are doing things RIGHT and point
    that out, acknowledging a great performance.
    This definitely doesn't mean praising their
    players for everything they do, but praise for a
    good play builds self-esteem and that is needed.

2. Understand differences in their athletes: The
    reality is that all players, especially young
    players, react differently to different coaching
    or management tactics. An excellent coach
    can identify this and find a way to coach to the
    players' strengths and handle each player in a
    way to maximize their performance. If the team
    has a highly-skilled player who does not handle
    being screamed at on a regular basis, there needs
    to be another way to motivate this kid. This is
    not an easy task. Many college lacrosse programs
    have 35-60 players on the roster, and this means
    a wide variety of personalities. But, in order to
    be a great coach, they must identify each player's

strengths and weaknesses, both physically and mentally.

3. Able to connect with each person: Young athletes are often sensitive to how they are dealt with, but one thing that is almost always a certainty us that the best teams want to play for their coach. In my time as an athlete, I have found that I am able to play my best with the trust of my coach. Accountability is necessary, but when it comes down to it, the best teams want to win for their coach. When the going gets tough, players who are close with their coach can handle the toughness and push through. On the other hand, if a game or season takes a turn for the worse, the teams who feel disconnected with their coach often never dig themselves out of that hole.

Ex. My freshman year of college: Georgetown vs. Notre Dame out in Indiana. After a not so hot year for Georgetown the year before (4-10 record to be exact), the odds were definitely not in our favor to win the game. So, leading up to the game there was definitely some nerves, especially considering the game was on TV. After a solid fall performance in the goal, I was named the starter for the Hoyas. I typically was not one to get nervous before games because I'm naturally a pretty mellow person, but this game was different. Because it was my first game ever playing at the college level, I couldn't help but feel the nerves. As we stood in the locker room listening to music before the game, I paced around trying to stay loose and active. Before he gave his speech, my head coach came up to me. He looked at me with a straight face and calmly said to me, "Nicky you know you're our guy. You'll be great out there". Although it was just a few simple words, in that moment I knew my coach trusted me and he had my back. That gave me the confidence I needed to go out there any do my thing. Although we lost by 2 goals, I played very well and had 12 saves, a couple of which were big time saves, to keep it a close game.

4. Accountability: It is great to have a coach you can connect with and be able to learn from on a personal level. At the same time, there is a winner and a loser at the end of every game. The team, including both the coaches and players, must be accountable for themselves and for their

peers. No team is going to find success by having a coach who is nice all the time. The best coaches certainly find their fair share of times when they get after their players and be tough on them, but when they have the team's trust and respect that tough love is a key ingredient the team needs. The best coaches will not let any "bs" fly, and their players will know the reasoning behind it all. It is the balance that makes a coach great. It does not really matter the level you are coaching at because if you can connect to players on a personal level while holding them accountable, success will eventually come.

The all-time leader in lacrosse wins, Mike Messere, is a perfect example of this coaching style. Now a member of the National Lacrosse Hall of Fame, Messere wrestled and played lacrosse at Cortland State University before graduating in 1966 and starting his coaching legacy. With a 757-55 record in 37 years, Messere has the highest winning record of any high school or college coach. He has led West Genesee (NY) to become a powerhouse for lacrosse. His team have won a national record 15 state championships with six runner-up finishes, amounting to winning 93% of his games. Wow! That's pretty good in my book.

What is even more impressive about his coaching career is the amount of players who went on to play at the college level. That is a testament to his strength as a coach but also as an advocate for the game of lacrosse. Let's be honest, there are not many players out there, especially young kids, who will feel driven to continue their athletic careers if they're playing for a bad coach. Now, to say Messere was not tough would be a lie because many alumni would say otherwise. But he developed discipline in his players and they wanted to play for him. Out of all of his years of coaching, Messere had only had 8 players not go on to play at the college level. 8! And even more remarkable is that more than 100 former players have gone on to coach lacrosse at some level.

There have been many players from West Genesee who have gone on to play at Syracuse, a powerhouse program at the D1 level. In fact, 7 of the starters of their first NCAA champion team in 1983 were from West Genesee. The current coach of the Orange, John Desko (West Genesee alum), is outspoken about his admiration for the coaching style and success of Mike Messere. "He taught me lacrosse. He's best described as a teacher. He's very big on fundamentals and discipline. The way he teaches the game, he's not going to lose a lot. Some of the things we do at Syracuse, I learned from Mike."

A pretty funny story that Desko remembers from his days at West Genesee paints a good picture of the Messere way. As he explained, one of their players showed up late to practice one day. Apparently the player had been out hunting, causing him to be late to practice. To prove his point to the player and obviously to the whole team as well, Messere told the player to bring the bird he had shot to practice the next day. That next day, Messere had the bird's wings wrapped around the player's helmet for the entirety of the practice.

Messere's style is to stress to his players that success is all about the process. You bought into the program or you hit the road. Mike Buzzell, another former West Genny player, vividly recalls the effects that playing for Messere had on him. Buzzell has had quite the career both on and off the field. A member of the National Hall of Fame, Buzzell went on to be a Top Gun Navy fighter pilot and has flown for FedEx for 25 years. Although he only had Messere as a coach for his senior season, he took a lot out of that one year. "He gets kids to show up at 5 in the morning for practice. They practice a lot on their own. It's definitely an art and a skill in this day and age. Winning came from buying into the program. You were going to win if you accepted the process. He's a top-notch teacher of leadership. That type of approach carried with me through college and in the Navy. We all come back to support Mike. I think the world of the guy."

Talk about accountability...this guy really emphasized it. Buzzell remembers a game in which the Wildcats didn't play their best, and coach Messere made it known. "On the way home, he stopped the bus and we had to run the (Westcott) Reservoir," Buzzell said. "It's not like a mountain, but you have to run to the top and it's dark. That opened our eyes and was kind of the turning point in the season." That team finished with a 19-1 record.

That reservoir has seen its fair share of Messere moments. After one loss in a season Buzzell was not a part of, Messere took the team to the reservoir, got them off the bus, and began 'lecturing' them. After a few minutes, Messere told the team they weren't good enough to run the reservoir, as if it were a reward. And that is exactly what is has come to be - a reward. After every state championship win, the team stops at that same reservoir. Players, coaches, and ex-players all run to the top of the hill as a reward.

At first glance it seems like Messere could be a bit of a crazy, winning obsessed madman, but that is certainly not the case. He truly cares about all his players, off the field as well as on. Bob Deegan, the assistant coach who has been monumental in the success of West Genny along with Messere, gave a taste of the head coach's handling of his players. Recalling one of the better players to play at West Genny, Messere said how "he was a real good, tough kid, but he had this thing about school, kind of giving us lip service. Mike took a small school desk and put it in the corner of the field. In full uniform he had to do his homework. He had to show it to us and have each teacher initial it. He finally got the message and (later made All—America) and was Cum Laude in college." (Maxpreps)

As if he had not done enough to bring success to the West Genny high school program, Messere was instrumental in developing a youth program at Shove Park. Desko addressed this by saying - "I think (he was) one of the first guys to really organize all the levels underneath him and kind of teach the other coaches that he's had, working with the younger guys." The importance of developing a strong youth program was important to Messere and would be important for the success of the high school team along the way. Players in 1st through 10th grade were considered the feeder program and juniors and seniors were considered the high school team. With this system, only five freshmen have ever played varsity for coach Messere.

Mike Messere's coaching legacy has attracted attention across the lacrosse community and many coaches at every level try to emulate his ways, even some of the greats like John Desko at Syracuse. It is remarkable how much success he has brought the lacrosse community of West Genesee, but also to the players old and new who continue to thrive as both players and people.

TAKEAWAYS:

- Developing a high level college team is not easy: there are rules to abide by (at least in the US) and it can be costly. Something to consider for a country just adopting the sport is setting up club teams. There will be much less restriction for club and the transition can eventually be made to a higher level.

- Find the right coaches: once a program has been developed at the university level, you must find an adequate leader to develop these players on and off the field.(See coaching qualities above)

- Follow the Mike Messere path: Aim for a coach like Messere. He knew how to challenge and get the best out of his players while developing lasting and meaningful connections. This was huge in his success as a coach.

CHAPTER 8

HOW RUSSIA CREATED A DOMINATING SPORTS PROGRAM—THAT ANOTHER COUNTRY COULD MODEL THEIR PROGRAMS ON

———

Russia has always been very strong in sports, especially when it was known as the USSR. During the Soviet Era, the USSR national team placed 1st in total medals won in 14 of the 18 Olympic appearances. Quite a significant stat right there! One sport in particular that Russia and the USSR has enjoyed tremendous success with is ice hockey.

Some of the best players in the sport hail from Russia: Alexander Ovechkin, Viacheslav Fetisov and Vladislav Tretyak are just a few. "Fetisov was the heart and soul of the great Soviet teams of the 1980s and a huge advocate that Russian players gain the freedom to play outside the Soviet Union, namely in the NHL. Tretyak is a legendary goalie, a 10-time World Champion, 3-time Olympic champion and 1-time Canada Cup champion. He is also the only modern-era non-NHL player in the Hockey Hall of Fame— one of only two Russian players so honored." Alexander Ovechkin, the most known one of the three because of his dominance while playing in the US, has set records on records and currently leads a talented Washington Capitals team.

But it is no coincidence that some of the greatest hockey players come from Russia. Actually, it is pretty much the opposite. It's almost destiny for many players raised in this system. Since birth, many Russians are essentially bred to be hockey gods.

Before WWII, there was actually no ice hockey in Russia. Instead, they played a game called bandy, which would help develop a new style of hockey the world had never seen before. The best way to explain bandy is that it is essentially soccer on ice. There are 11 players on each team, and the game is played with a small round ball. It is played on a rink that is 110 yards long and 60 yards wide, similar to that of a soccer field. Similar to hockey, the objective of the game is to use your stick to hit the ball in the opposing team's net. The difference is that the net is much larger in bandy that that of ice hockey. This game became the guide for what would become ice hockey in Russia.

Playing off finesse rather than physicality, the Russians brought a new style that was not seen from the likes of the Canadians or the Americans. It was around 1946 that the first Russian hockey league was created and thus began the new era of ice hockey. Thought of as the father of Russian hockey, Anatoli Tarasov described the game as if it was an art, stating "A hockey player must have the wisdom of a chess player, the accuracy of a sniper and the rhythm of a musician." Just eight years after the sport was introduced, the Soviet team played in its first world championships in 1954, going undefeated and defeating Canada 7-2 in the championship game. Just 8 years! "The Soviet Union took its sports very seriously during the Cold War. Each gold medal, each world record, each triumph was seen as just that, a triumph of Soviet dominance. It was that way in space. It was that way in the arts. And it was particularly that way in hockey. The Soviets won 22 world championships and eight Olympic gold medals and, even more, won them with style and finesse and a flair that was exclusively Russian". (WashingtonPost)

Because of the breakup of the Soviet Union, the pure dominance in hockey declined but Russia was still looked at as a powerhouse in the sport, just as it was as the USSR. If you have ever seen the movie Miracle, you should know this. The USSR was scary. They were on another level and were nearly unstoppable, that was until Mike Eruzione and the 1980 Olympic team stopped that run in maybe the most memorable sports moment ever. "When they got it going," American Mike Eruzione would say, "it wasn't even hockey. It was like ballet or something. You would be on the ice watching them just like the fans." That level of hockey has diminished since the Soviet Union split and since players just started chasing the money, but getting back on track here, how did the Soviet Union get so good at hockey in such a short period of time?

It is actually quite amazing how the Russians were able to create such dominance in a sport while going through the Cold War. Life there wasn't how it is today. Resources were very scarce but that didn't stop any Russian family from trying to breed their young child into the next big star.

One of the all-time greatest in the NHL, Evgeni Malkin, came from Russia and grew up in the land of ice hockey.

"Now kids are equipped with everything, while back then we had to mend the uniform 10 times," Vladimir says. "That's how many times my wife had to do it! ...And then it would rip again. The socks, the gloves also – his hands were cut up. Nothing has remained from all that equipment. No one knew that he'd play so well." (Mccollough, Post-Gazette)

The current Pittsburgh Penguins forward grew up in the town of Magnitogorsk, where either you could play hockey all day, or work in the factory. Malkin chose the rink. In 1989, at the age of 3, Malkin began skating, and by the age of 6 was already in group-leagues, the youngest one to play in the league by around 1 or 2 years.

Growing out of communist ideas, the town of Magnitogorsk screamed industrialization, and demanded a lot out of its people. No matter who you were or who you knew, you would have equal work and equal pay working in the factories.

Evgeni Malkin was fortunate enough to grow up with a father who loved the sport of hockey and who knew the potential that was there with his son. Vladamir Malkin grew up with a father who worked as a driver of heavy vehicles, and he himself went to school and learned to play hockey. Although

Vladamir was given the chance to play the sport in the Soviet Union, there was no real potential for him. "The Metallurg Magnitogorsk hockey team had begun in the 1950s, but it was just a club program. The Soviets outlawed professional sports, seeing them as emblematic of the greed that plagued the West. Metallurg did not have its own arena. For a boy, there was no life in hockey, no matter how much of a desire he had." (Mccollough, Post-Gazette)

Despite the hardships, Vladimir Malkin never once complained or stopped working hard. Instead, he worked even harder and sought out the best for his family. He worked tirelessly to provide for the four people in the household and was the only one working. One thing he could provide from his past was his hockey knowledge.

When Evgeni was 5 years old, Vladimir put him in the Metallurg Magnitogorsk hockey school. At this point you are probably wondering why you are reading so much about a Russian hockey player when this book is all about lacrosse. But, looking deeper into his life, you can get an idea as to why he was so successful and why the Russians have developed such dominant players in the sport. It is this process that must be evaluated, because although this was done solely in hockey, this process can be used elsewhere with other sports.

When Vladimir was young, they did not even have a proper arena to play at. Then, in 1991, the Ivan Romazan Ice Palace opened just a few city blocks from the Malkins' 10-story apartment building. This was when the opportunities opened up, especially for a young Evgeni. Ivan Romazan was the president of the Magnitogorsk Steel and Iron Works and shared a love for sports, eager to produce a sports arena in the area. In 1993, future plant president Viktor Rashnikov pushed major investments into the Metallurg franchise, including more resources devoted to the hockey school.

Evgeni, along with a group of about 60 others, began waking up at 6am every day to go to the arena to play hockey. They were eager to play the game, and found a way to do so, playing before elementary school as well as after. For these youngsters, it was all about hockey. They had two choices: succeed in hockey or go work in the factory. This passion for the sport was developed within these young players and it simply could not be taken from them. They did not come from much, but that did not stop them. Evgeni's mother, Natalia, once went upstairs to check on Evgeni, only to find him sound asleep with a goalie mask on his head. This love for hockey drove him, which was why he was brought up to play with the older group of kids.

Although much of Evgeni's success can be attributed to the help of his family and especially his father, much of it was also due to the team he was playing with and the nurturing and coaching he was given. With the help of Rashnikov's money, the Metallurg Magnitogorsk youth team traveled far to places like Chicago and San Francisco to capture championships.

"To grow one good player in hockey, you have to be training 25 people on the team. You need to go on trips and play games with other teams. You must give them the equipment, which is deteriorating rapidly, feed them and keep the coaching staff. Parents for hockey school almost do not pay. The basic costs are borne by the hockey club and help from the plant. It's a very, very, very hard and long job." (Post-Gazette)

There were nearly 500 kids in one year in the same hockey school. They were all there to make it big and were determined to do so. They were there to become stars. For many players during that time, the pressure to stay and play in Russia was very intense. Luckily for Evgeni, he made an escape to the United States, a move that enraged his Russian hockey club and more so Rashnikov. But one year after arriving in the United States, the move proved to be a smart one, as he had a breakout year in the National Hockey League.

But, before his time, life was not as easy. A member of the Hockey Hall of Fame and a major influencer in breaking the barrier that kept Soviet players from playing in the NHL, Igor Larionov told his story about his life as a Soviet hockey player.

At the age of 19, following the 1980 Olympics that were so well known from the movie "Miracle", Larionov was recruited to play for CSKA Moscow, aka the Soviet "Red Army" National Team. During this time, every young man had to serve two years in the army and there was no getting around that. For him and many others, in the Red Army he was a hockey player and nothing else. 25 players trained for 11 months straight. They practiced four hours a day and did off-ice training for another 5-6 hours a day. Following that, they would typically watch film for another two hours. No days off. The conditions at camp were not particularly great. They lived in barrack-like rooms and had no time outside of playing hockey.

Life was rough during this Cold War Period and the hockey rink became a way for players to express themselves. Not to say this system of training was in any ways "right" or fair, but it worked.

They were obsessed with the sport. The government, the fans, the players - all obsessed. But that success in the Soviet Union would begin to diminish. The Soviet players began to row angry at Coach Viktor Tikhonov's tyrannical ways and soon sought to play elsewhere. "After their 1980 defeat by the Americans, the players were sequestered from their families and training intensified. The Soviet team won gold medals in the 1984 and 1988 Olympics. But the players despised Tikhonov and, like their nation, grew disenchanted as the Soviet Union buckled and dissolved."(Documentary.org) After much backlash, Soviet players were allowed to play in Canada and the U.S., which became the downfall of Soviet hockey as it was known.

Aside from the downfall of the Soviet Union following the Cold War Era, the potential for hockey to continue to flourish was right there. Players were bred to play the sport and given all the opportunities to be their best, but it came with no choice. Still, it was this structure and the growth of their players that made the Soviet teams so successful.

Soviet organizations put kids on skates at a much earlier age than other powerful countries such as Canada and the US. Even as early as 3, players were taught to skate, making their 'on ice hockey sense' develop that much sooner. Players were encouraged to be creative and skillful. Players were confined to spending their every hour playing hockey, thinking hockey, and talking hockey. Nearly 11 hours a day! As crazy as it sounds, this method proved successful in that it isolated players and forced them to focus solely on the ice and the puck. Players stuck together for years, playing with the same group of teammates every year. This created real teams instead of just individual players. That style of play has for the most part disappeared in Russia, which is quite obvious since the Russians have been unsuccessful in International play since the Soviet Union days.

Along with this, the coaches that were present during the Soviet Union era were top of the line and were there to bring out the best of each player. In the 1990s, a declining Russia was forced to get rid of funding for hockey schools. Due to the dedication to the sport, many devoted coaches stayed aboard and talented players still came through. But that later declined and because of a lack of money, there are not as many great coaches as in the past. "During the Soviet days there was a strong foundation of coaches, which supported everything. But that generation of coaches is gone and the generation of their students is also gradually disappearing." (Documentary.org)

Funding played a major role in the success of Soviet players and the Soviet national team. "In the Soviet era, top talents like Fetisov were drafted into the military with the express purpose of playing for the Red Army club, which in turn fed the national team." "Basically the whole system was funded by the government," Polsky explains." (<u>Documentary.org</u>)

The country of Russia now is much different from the Soviet Union of the past, for good and bad reasons. And regardless of how they were viewed politically, there was no arguing that their national sports programs were a model of success. They did breed amazing athletes. They knew how to run a system that in turn won medals and championships. But they did not know when to stop. The treatment of their athletes was not fair. They had bits and pieces of the ideal system in place, but in the end their communist views were too much to sustain that much success.

The whole point of this? If you look at what the Soviet Union did - they created a masterpiece. They developed a program from scratch and made it into the best the world had for a long, long time. They developed schools for players to focus on playing hockey and put government funds into it so these players would have the best coaches and the ability to play all day, every day. Players were encouraged to be creative and play with "freedom" on the ice, ironically enough given the communist ways during that time.

This structure worked for hockey, but it could also be adopted and used in any other sport. Nobody quite knows why the Soviet Union decided to develop hockey as its premier sport, but it did. And it worked.

KEY TAKEAWAYS:

- Russians were introduced to hockey at a very young age. This is crucial for the success of a new sport.

- Though players were often constricted under the Soviet regime, players saw hockey as an opportunity. This needs to be stressed when presenting lacrosse to new players.

- The Soviet hockey teams received support through government funding. This was significant for the success of their teams.

CHAPTER 9

THE NEW VISION

—

Lacrosse in Russia - a premier sport in the country. Russians in general are currently very unfamiliar with the sport, despite it recently being admitted into the Federation of International Lacrosse (FIL) and for the first time playing in the world championships in 2014 in Denver. Its first showing did not go too well. The team went 2-6, finishing in 32nd place. Its only wins were against Argentina and Spain, two countries not known to have any relevance in the lacrosse world.

RUSSIA'S ROSTER FOLLOWS:

24 – Eugene Arkhipov – M – Moscow Lacrosse Club / RIT

6 – Aleksandr Avramenko – M – Moscow Lacrosse Club

0 – Aleksei Chernyshov – G – Moscow Lacrosse Club

2 – Zachary Cowan – A – Kent Denver (CO)

22 – David Diamonon – A – Kyiv Bulava Lacrosse (Ukraine) / St. John's School (TX)

40 – Nikolay Efimov – D – Moscow Lacrosse Club

10 – Gavriel Egiazarov – M – Moscow Lacrosse Club

8 – Jordan Friedman – LSM/D – Colgate University

29 – Travis Karpak – D – Chicago Outlaws

1 – Dmitrii Khamin – M – Moscow Lacrosse Club

38 – Nick Koshansky – M – Notre Dame

28 – Will Koshansky – LSM – Rochester Rattlers / University of Pennsylvania

20 – Philipp Le – D – Northfield Mount Hermon (MA)

17 – Jacob Richards – D – Salisbury School (CT)

7 – Nicholas Rjedkin – A/M – Brookdale Community College

13 – Valerii Severukhin – D/LSM – Moscow Lacrosse Club

33 – Alexey Sukhanov – D – Moscow Lacrosse Club

11 – Alec Tilley – A – Belleville Township High School (IL)

16 – Artur Ventsel – A/M – Moscow Lacrosse Club

32 – Drew Zambelli – G – Moscow Lacrosse Club / Oberlin College

42 – Alexander Zarubin – D – Moscow Lacrosse Club

31 – Artem Zarubin – D – Moscow Lacrosse Club

9 – Ray Zimlin – G – Manhattanville College

HEAD COACH:

Peter Milliman, Cornell University

ASSISTANT COACHES:

Joe Cuozzo, Cortland State University, National Lacrosse Hall of Fame, Class of 1992

John Foley, Team Ontario / RIT

Rick Mercurio, Sachem High School (NY) / Rutgers

Mike Thumim, Dakota Ridge High School (CO) / Ohio University

Dan Willson, Greater Birmingham Youth Lacrosse Association (AL) / Thomas Jefferson High School for Science and Technology (VA)

Despite having quite am impressive lineup of coaches, all having lacrosse experience at a high level, the Russian team proved to be unsuccessful. So why focus on Russia? As crazy as it sounds, it is an ideal country for a new and developing sport to thrive. Russia has proven to be competitive in everything they take part in, all the way from politics to athletics. Some of the time, the two even intertwine. Even more so, the Russian government takes great pride in their sports and whether or not they are perceived as dominant.

In the 2016 Summer Olympics in Brazil, lacrosse again was not included as a sport. It was then announced that baseball, karate, skateboarding, softball, sport climbing and surfing would be added to the 2020 Summer Olympics in Tokyo. After the FIL was accepted to SportAccord in 2012, and the International World Games Association in 2013, it has been making steps to be again a part of the Summer Olympics. It has formally applied to the International Olympic Committee. The FIL is doing what it needs to be admitted as an Olympic sport and it is looking likely that lacrosse will soon be an Olympic sport again, an encouraging development for any country promoting or developing the sport.

As far as the Russian economy goes, it has been on a surprisingly positive trend. When Vladimir Putin became president, Russia essentially went bankrupt as it owed more money to the International Monetary Fund (IMF) than it had in foreign currency reserves. Since then it has become one of the largest creditors of US debt in the world. It's GDP has been on the rise and the economy seems to be holding stable, creating a more hopeful climate for Russians.

Since Putin's rule, he has gone to great measures to make Russian athletics the best of the best. The Russian government puts a lot of resources into "fitness" and sports. In reality, the government puts funds into the sports it feels can win and win a lot.

"The Ministry of Sport (Minsport) is a federal executive body responsible for drafting and implementing government policy and legal regulation in physical fitness and sport, providing state services (including anti-doping measures), and managing public property in the area of physical fitness and sport." (government.ru)

In 2008, Vitaly Mutko was appointed the Russian Ministry of Sport, Tourism, and Youth Policy. He plays a major role in the funding of Russian athletics and more specifically those Olympic sports.

David Diamonon was the first person to introduce lacrosse to the Russian community when he moved to Moscow in 2007. He was first introduced to lacrosse when he was teaching in Houston, Texas, and after a few years of losing contact with the sport he came to love, he picked it up again. After being sent to Russia for work, he decided to start a team. From his efforts, there are now two teams in Russia: the Moscow Rebels and the St. Petersburg White Knights. They play each other twice a year, and the winner is champion of Russia. The issue is that most of the teams are made up of Americans who are living in Russia. "We have a growing number of pure Russian players. That really is the point. If this is going to live on, it has to be people who live here. This has got to be Russians," he told RBTH. Another problem with the existing setup is that most of the players are ages 19-25, which means there is little, if any youth involvement.

There are a lot of steps necessary for the sport to make an impact in Russia. First, there needs to be a bottom-up approach. What this means is there needs to be youth involvement if there is going to be long-term success. If we take a look at the World Games, many of the players on the Russian National Team are players from America. Without a youth program put in place, the sport is going nowhere. As Mike Messere showed with his development of West Genny, developing a youth program made a major impact in the high school program winning down the road. Without it, it is nearly impossible.

STEPS TO SUCCESS

1. Hire a team of coaches and directors

2. Implement a youth program within schools - a combination of the LTN model and Laxachusetts

3. Expand lacrosse into the high school age level

4. Start creating athletic specific lacrosse schools – And secure more funding to do so.

5. National level - Need a strong program to develop the National Team

STEP 1: HIRING A TEAM TO DEVELOP THE SPORT:

This step will be hugely important in regards to expanding the game in Russia. Having a real lacrosse presence in Russia is critical in order to grow the game. It is important to have a strong group of coaches and directors to take this program in the right direction. For example, Laxachusetts was created by a group of people with a lot of experience in lacrosse and who were all totally committed to develop the best club program in the state of Massachusetts. It is crucial to find someone in Russia who has experience with lacrosse to build the organization and infrastructure. David Diamonon would be a perfect choice to fill this role but since he left to go to Ukraine for work that is not possible. Yevgeny Arkhipov took over as head coach of the Moscow Rebels after Diamonon's departure and is someone who can provide great insight as to the culture of the Russian people and how to get things done within the political system there. Additional personnel with lacrosse knowledge need to be recruited to make lacrosse a national sport.

STEP 2: IMPLEMENT A YOUTH PROGRAM IN MOSCOW

This is not going to be easy by any means. The fact that almost no one knows what the sport of lacrosse is will obviously make it difficult to recruit young players. Not too many young athletes will be eager to get out on a field and throw a rubber ball around with a stick. Implement the game with one local school. Expose the young athletes in that school to the game through clinics and exhibitions. Show them lacrosse on TV or recordings of American high school and college lacrosse games. Expose them to the gear used to play lacrosse. In order to do this, resources will be necessary, which is certainly not an easy task and will clearly need the support of local government leaders.

Funding is huge. On the first trip to any school you will need to bring equipment. Sticks are the number one priority. There are currently approximately 50 people playing lacrosse in Moscow, Russia according to David Diamonon and none of them are youth players. To begin there's a need for about

30 sticks that will cost $70 each, a cost of $2100 in lacrosse sticks alone to get started.

That helps transition into the next point, which deals with actually introducing the game and understanding the culture of these people. As Lacrosse The Nations made a point to do, it is important to realize the bigger picture here. You are going in to implement a youth lacrosse league in Russia but at the end of the day, Russia does not NEED lacrosse. It is easy for the Russians to swiftly say no to lacrosse. First and foremost is connecting with the people and through that you will be able to start a youth program. Once you have actually started to gain some ground and have a group of youth players to start with, remember these kids know nothing about the game of lacrosse. Start slow!

MONTH 1:

The first few weeks will be tough as you will lose and gain players every day. Start by teaching the basics. Teach the kids how to catch and throw and implement the proper throwing techniques. From there you can work on things like ground balls and some shooting. Start with 3 sessions per week for the first month and evaluate how each week goes: The good, the bad, and what to change.

MONTH 2-4:

After the first month, there will be more youth involvement. If kids are encouraged by playing lacrosse, talk to the school and try to set up a PE lacrosse session. This would be huge in bringing in more kids to play and retaining players in the program. As long as this goes as planned, you can bump up the number of sessions from 3 to 4 per week. Again, harp on the little things: Proper technique and discipline. Start incorporating small games to retain interest of players and let them have fun with it.

After the two months of the program is over, you need to really take a step back and evaluate. To keep the program going, you are going to need more funding and it will most likely need to come from a donor. Think about what some of the nonprofits did in regard to their funding. LTN was able to get donations from lacrosse companies such as Lacrosse Unlimited. Without this funding, it will be hard to continue to run the program and account for the equipment, coaching salaries, as well as facility costs.

STEP 3: EXPANDING LACROSSE AT THE HIGH SCHOOL AGE

Once a strong youth league has been implemented in Moscow, you will need to make the transition from youth into high school. If developing a youth league wasn't hard enough, developing a high school league will be even harder. Retention is going to be the key in order to start a strong program at the high school level.

A lot of this should be taken care of already if the youth program that you set up operated correctly. In order to start a league within schools, there will need to be a lot of cooperation with the local schools. There will need to be more than one school with a full rostered team so that teams are able to have a schedule of games. Because of this, it would make more sense to start a high school level program outside of the school.

LTN did something similar with their program. They incorporated both a program within the school as well as one that was after school. This made sense for them so that they could have more time to spend with kids and so kids who were not enrolled in school could play. For the Russian league, it would be the best idea to first have an out of school program.

STEP 4:

Next, think about the Soviet Union Regime. The way the Soviets trained their athletes, especially their hockey players, they were set up for success. Combine what the Soviets did with their hockey program and what IMG does with their athletics. IMG does a tremendous job of focusing on the total athlete, meaning the athlete on the field and off the field. At the same time, this is much easier to do with just one school full of kids. If lacrosse in Russia is going to flourish at the high school aged level, there will need to be much more exposure than just one IMG-like school. There will need to be plans to recruit the best players and have the best coaches at "sports academies" across the country. What made the Soviets so successful in hockey had a lot to do with the coaches they had in their system. They were a major reason for the success on the ice during that era.

Funding athletics focused schools is going to require a lot of money. This time around, a Lacrosse Unlimited is not going to do the trick. The benefit of starting lacrosse in Russia is the possibility of receiving government funding. Vladimir Putin has been an advocate for sports being a major role in schools in Russia and has even made an effort to fund athletics in Russia. A federal funding program was set to operate from 2016-2020 and would replace the pre-existing athletic scheme. The 73.9 billion ruble ($1.8 billion) program was created to promote physical activity and increase the number of school-level sports competitions. Putin spoke about the dynamics of sports, stating "I believe, [sport] competitions between schools are very interesting and unite the children around their teams."(Nick Butler, Insidethegames.biz)

If you aren't convinced that lacrosse can be one of these sports being funded by the government, think again. One thing that needs to be understood about Russia is that a win in sports, especially at the Olympic Games, is seen as a political victory as well. Consider the 1980 Olympic Games for instance. The Olympic Games represented a whole lot more than just a medal. It showed who the leading power in the world was and in this case with hockey, the USSR had been dominant prior to 1980. After the Miracle on Ice, the United States took this as a political victory and the USSR was severely defeated. "It enhances the reputation of the administration, even though it had nothing to do with it. Simply, citizens bathed in the glow [of the win] that somehow capitalism, Americans [and] the free world had won some type of significant, symbolic victory." The Soviet Union was embarrassed by this loss and even to this day do not like to speak about that game. After the loss, many of the veteran Soviet players were cut and a new team was brought in.

Fast forward to present day and there is obviously a much different political system in place but the mindset is still similar. The drive to win is high and the Russians still feel winning in sports is a way to succeed on the big stage. Putin and Russia puts money into sports that will win and make Russia look good. If lacrosse proves to be a sport that could do exactly that, there is not a doubt that the Russian government would put money into the sport.

In 2016, the Russian government put $30 million into a complex for acrobatic rock'n'roll. It will be built on the western outskirts of Moscow and is funded by the municipal government. "The 1-acre complex is being built for the Moscow City Khamovniki state sports and dance school— where Tikhonova studied—and will be the only specialized facility in the world dedicated to the niche sport, according to the World Rock'n'Roll Confederation (WRRC)." (Nick Butler, Insidethegames.biz) Funny enough, it is actually Putin's youngest daughter's favorite sport. Katerina Tikhonova, 30, and her dance partner Dmitry Alekseev are ranked the 11th-best rock n' rollers in the world and sixth-best in Russia. The best way to describe the "sport" is that it involves couples dancing to rock music and mixing in acrobatic flips and stunts. The sport does not even appeal to most of the public. It is a couples sport. But still, an enormous amount of money was put into the sport for arguably personal reasons. The funding is certainly available and the Russian government, especially under Putin, is willing to invest resources into sports that will bring the country success.

Receiving adequate resources and funding will take some time. It is not going to happen overnight, or even in the first few years of introducing lacrosse in Russia. With the help of people like Moscow Rebels head coach Yevgeny Arkhipov, the game can make its mark in Russia, but a methodical approach must be taken.

STEP 5: STRUCTURING THE NATIONAL TEAM

Once all of the pieces have been put in place on the lower levels, it will be time to develop a strong National Team. There is a solid foundation to work on in regards to the National Team. Russia was admitted to the Federation of International Lacrosse and participated in the 2014 World Games. Even though they had a poor showing, it shows potential in the sport for the Russians and easier access to developing a strong foundation at the national level.

Hiring a strong coach will be critical for the growth of the players as well as the national program as whole. The best way to do this is to use the "Mike Messere Model". Messere had a great balance of being a coach who was tough as nails as well as a respected person off the field. He demanded a lot from his players and because of that they played their hearts out for him. Messere's knowledge of the game of lacrosse was beyond that of most coaches and because of that, he brought a lot of success to the West Genny program. Although it will be rare to find a coach that can stack up against a coach and leader like Mike Messere, that is what the goal should be.

In 2014, there was a lot of involvement with the National Team from experienced players and coaches of the game. The head coach for the Russian team during the world games in 2014 was Peter Milliman, who was a defensive coordinator at Cornell University. A three-time All-American at Gettysburg and former Major League Lacrosse player with Rochester, Milliman was also an assistant coach at Princeton, R.I.T. and Siena, and spent four years as the head coach at Pfeiffer College. Also on the coaching staff was National Lacrosse Hall of Famer Joe Cuozzo, who won over 700 games as a high school coach in New York. These are two candidates who have already experienced coaching the Russian Team and who could provide a great foundation to developing a dynasty.

2032 OLYMPIC GAMES LACROSSE CHAMPIONSHIP: USA VS. RUSSIA

Two teams line up for the opening draw. On one side are the familiar faces of the United States team - Paul Rabil, Scott Ratliff, Joel White, Drew Adams, and John Galloway among others. The US team is stacked with talent just as they have been year after year. What is unique on this day is the team that the US is facing on the other side of the faceoff X. They have the usual red and white as is seen in nearly every championship battle between Canada and the US, but this team has a different name across their chests. The US is facing Team Russia, a team that has built their program from scratch and years later are playing with the best of the best. Unlike their first World Games appearance in 2014, this Olympic Russian team is full of native Russian players who have been playing for years in the same league that started in Moscow. They graduated from the youth leagues in Moscow funded by the Russian government along with major businesses thriving in a growing global economy. They then furthered their skills on their club team against top competition from across Russia, Europe and North America, including against their greatest rival the USA. Then after being recognized as being amongst the best of the best in Russia, they were invited to attend the National Sports Academy in Moscow, where they further honed their skills, balancing a full academic workload along with practices and training sessions headed up by the sport's most elite coaches. Not to mention they travel all over Europe and North America to play the top University, High School and Prep School teams. All of this in the quest to be one of the elite few to be invited to try out for the Russian National Team that would represent their homeland in the Olympic Games. But here they were, about to do just that. Playing a game that their parents had never even heard of before they began to play as 5 year olds. What an incredible journey it had been to get here.

Let the Games begin!

ACKNOWLEDGEMENTS

—

First off, I would like to thank my entire family, who have watched me grow as a lacrosse player, and quite honestly placed me into the sport. Mom, Dad, Lex, Erica: You guys are especially awesome. I cannot thank you enough for always being by my side and gifting me with the ability to publish this book. I have always had a hidden passion for writing but have not had the opportunity to take advantage of it.

Going off of that, I am extremely grateful to Eric Koester and Brian Bies for pushing me forward through this process and never allowing me to let up. Without you both, this experience would not have been possible and I thank you for that. I also want to thank Anastasia Armendariz and Catherine Schluth for all their help in editing and providing me with great feedback to take this book to the next level.

I would also like to say a big thanks to Michaela Bruno, Mikey Doyle, and my dad for constantly reading over my work. I know you all have busy lives but I appreciate all your feedback and am extremely happy you all were a part of this process. Tucker Gillman, Dan Bucaro, Matt Sharpe, Drew Hadley, Scott and Matt Whear, Massi Bucci, Stephen MacLeod, Adam Ghitelman, Tom Schreiber, Brett Hughes, Javier Silva, Spencer Riehl and many others: thank you all for providing a really cool spin on this book. I hope you guys enjoy being a part of it. In addition, I would like to thank the many great organizations that have done work teaching lacrosse both in the US and abroad, including Lacrosse The Nations, Kids Lacrosse The World, and Harlem Lacrosse.

Lastly, I want to thank my college teammates. You guys have all played a huge part in my experiences as a lacrosse player and a person and that has allowed me to ultimately write this book. I could not be more excited and will always remember all those amazing times.

I hope this book helps us find the next Nick Marrocco living in South Africa, Brazil, Japan, or Kenya so that he or she can fall in love with the sport of lacrosse too.

SOURCES USED

---

http://en.espn.co.uk/olympic-sports/sport/story/280229.html

http://www.post-gazette.com/sports/olympicfeatures/2014/02/09/Evgeni-Malkin-A-Russian-tale-with-roots-founded-in-ice-and-iron/stories/201402090133

http://www.anthem-sports.com/baseball-equipment.html?gclid=EAIaIQobChMI1Jvp3_q21gIVBweGCh0iRgRJEAAYASAAEgL3nvD_BwE

http://sportsstudio.net/how-much-a-complete-football-uniform-costs-youth-and-adult-prices/

https://www.theatlantic.com/entertainment/archive/2012/04/will-lacrosse-ever-go-mainstream/255690

http://www.baltimoresun.com/features/maryland-family/bal-picking-the-right-lacrosse-club-20140820-story.html

https://www.uslacrosse.org/about-the-sport/history

https://www.theatlantic.com/entertainment/archive/2012/04/will-lacrosse-ever-go-mainstream/255690/

https://www.theguardian.com/football/blog/2010/jul/06/world-cup-2010-uruguay-history

http://www.independent.co.uk/travel/americas/uruguay-football-team-argentina-euros-luis-suarez-a7125561.html

https://www.indiegogo.com/projects/join-team-colombia-help-us-get-to-the-world-lacrosse-championships#/

http://www.insidelacrosse.com/article/colombia-announces-final-roster-for-world-games/28968

http://www.nytimes.com/1984/03/19/sports/jim-brown-s-best-sport.html

http://www.kidslacrossetheworld.org

https://www.lacrossethenations.org

http://www.harlemlacrosse.org

http://gobonnies.sbu.edu/general/2016-17/releases/20170321n1yrqr

http://www.maxpreps.com/news/JqLNjaRNhUGr7WZNdg76sQ/mike-messere-is-king-of-lacrosse-coaches-with-757-wins,-15-state-titles.htm

https://www.washingtonpost.com/sports/olympics/russian-hockey-team-carries-expectations-of-entire-country-as-olympic-tournament-begins/2014/02/12/a71a84b4-93fa-11e3-9e13-770265cf4962_story.html?utm_term=.f1fc93418cc4

http://www.documentary.org/feature/red-army-recalls-glory-days-soviet-hockey

https://www.insidethegames.biz/articles/1023169/new-multi-billion-ruble-russian-sports-funding-programme-unveiled-by-vladimir-putin

http://government.ru/en/department/60/events/

http://www.insidelacrosse.com/article/international-gear-moscow-rebels/14462

Several Player and Organization Interviews